COLLECTING
SILVER
The Facts At Your Fingertips

COLLECTING
SILVER
The Facts At Your Fingertips

Jill Bace

Special Consultants:
Alexis Butcher
Juliet Nusser

Collecting Silver
The Facts At Your Fingertips

First published in Great Britain in 1999 by Miller's, an imprint of
Mitchell Beazley, both divisions of Octopus Publishing Group Ltd,
2–4 Heron Quays, Docklands, London E14 4JP
© 1999 Octopus Publishing Group Ltd
Reprinted 2000

Miller's is a registered trademark of Octopus Publishing Group Ltd

This edition distributed in the USA by Antique Collectors Club Ltd,
Market Street Industrial Park, Wappingers' Falls, New York,
NY 12590, USA

Commissioning Editor Liz Stubbs
Executive Art Editor Vivienne Brar
Editor Clare Peel
Designer Louise Griffiths
Picture Research Claire Gouldstone
Production Paul Hammond, Karen Farquhar
Illustrator Amanda Patton
Indexer Hilary Bird

The publishers will be grateful for any information that will assist
them in keeping future editions up to date. Although all reasonable
care has been taken in the preparation of this book, neither the
publishers nor the compilers can accept any liability for any
consequence arising from the use thereof, or the information
contained therein.

A CIP catalog record for this book is available
from the British Library

ISBN 1 84000 231 X
Set in Bembo
Produced by Toppan Printing Co., (HK) Ltd.
Printed and bound in China

Front cover *(Clockwise from top left)* Coffeepot by
Christian Wiltberger, *c*.1785, $15,200–24,800; William and
Mary candlestick, 1694, $13,120–19,200; Arts and Crafts
Timepiece, *c*.1900, $2,400–4,000; dish ring, 1912
$1,120–1,600; inkstand, 19thC, $3,200–4,800; entrée dish,
1815,$320–640; caddy spoon, 19thC, $160–240.
Front flap Flatware by Georg Jenson, *c*.1960,
$4,800–5,600 (for a 13-piece setting).
Back cover Tea service by Emil Viners, *c*.1935,
4,800–5,600.
Back flap Tankard, 1690s (with later decoration),
$1,600–3,200.
Page 2 *(Clockwise from top left)* Late Victorian enameled
vesta case, *c*.1880, $800–1,120; pierced dish in the 18thC

Dutch style by W. Comyns, 1901, $960–1,280;
1760s-style teapot by Charles Stuart Harris, 1897,
$480–640; French dwarf candelabrum, 19thC,
$1,600–2,400 (for a pair); George III swing-handled sugar
basket, 1796, $640–800; old Sheffield plate
salver, *c*.1835, $640–800; William IV coffeepot by
Garrards, 1832, $800–1,120; late Victorian "Swan"
cream jug, *c*.1880, $480–640.
Page 3 *(Clockwise from top left)* Punchbowl and ladle from
the Mackay service by Tiffany & Co., 1878,
$200,000–296,000; George II sauceboat, *c*.1740,
$960–1,120; enameled vesta case, early 20thC, $640–960;
Viennese ewer, *c*.1815, $1,280–1,600; George III tankard,
c.1790, $1,920–2,400

CONTENTS

INTRODUCTION

Few people are born with the proverbial silver spoon in their mouths. It is comparatively rare these days to be brought up surrounded by a household full of silver, whether eating breakfast from silver turnover dishes or egg cruets, taking afternoon tea from a silver service, or dining from silver flatware. To a degree, modern living hinders the owning and use of silver. Aspects of security, insurance, the care required to clean silver, and even the extra time required for the "rituals" of silver service mean that only a few privileged individuals enjoy its luxury.

Even if you were lucky enough to grow up with an abundance of silver and plated ware, it may still have passed you by unnoticed. Silver is a strange medium and people rarely treat it with indifference, tending either to love it or hate it. However, acquiring a love of silver is often merely a question of a catalyst sparking off what will inevitably turn into a passion.

My earliest recollections of silver at home are of my christening mug and a napkin ring, but even they were kept tucked away at the back of a sideboard drawer and rarely ever seen. Perhaps inspired by the mystery surrounding these items, I took a hallmark book from our bookshelves to find out more about the date letters. I remember the excitement on looking up the dates, and silverware then took on a magical appeal of hidden treasure.

I remember accompanying my mother and grandmother as a youngster to numerous church fêtes and bazaars, hoping to find a glittering piece of silver among the mediocre, lacklustre bits and bobs traditionally found on white elephant stalls. Even as a schoolboy I remember rummaging through a box of oddments on a secondhand bookstall at the market in my home town and finding to my amazement a silver teaspoon, recognizing the sterling lion passant through the grime. I naturally enquired the price of this gem and was told it would cost a penny. I duly purchased the spoon and continued looking through the box, only to be astonished when I found another silver teaspoon lying at the bottom of the box that not only matched the first one exactly but was also priced at a penny. Shortly afterwards I walked away from the stall with a set of six silver teaspoons, which had cost me a grand total of sixpence. This excitement that accompanies the discovery of a treasure is still something I experience today.

I remember taking these teaspoons to a silver dealer some years later. I was still a schoolboy and hence in school uniform. When I asked the dealer how much he would be prepared to give me for my spoons, he replied "seventeen pounds, but only, young man, on production of a letter of authority from your parents". The next day my parents duly obliged; I collected the money and was the richest boy in the school.

When you embark on collecting, silver will seem to be in short supply. It is not actually that scarce, but remember that it is all too easy to fritter away money, so be selective and patient. In fact, it is much wiser to spend $32 on a well-chosen reference book than to hastily buy a piece of silver. Build up a good library of reference books and absorb information from whatever sources you can. You may be on holiday, browsing in a bookshop for example, but be an opportunist. You can never have too many books. You may discover that one piece of knowledge gleaned is invaluable later on.

You should try and look at and handle as many pieces of silver as you can in order to be able to make comparisons of styles, quality and condition. Wherever possible, attend antiques fairs and regular silver auctions and visit dealers with large stocks – the London Silver Vaults in Chancery Lane for example. Try and visit public collections, museums, and galleries and not just in your own part of the world. Once you spread your interest you will probably find you develop certain tastes, and you may soon choose to hone in on a particular area that will have special interest to you. One of my favorite areas is early silver spoons (those dating from before 1700) and it is surprising when you delve into a narrow subject just how many people you meet with a similar interest and how large a subject it actually is. You may find that if you keep an open mind and are eager to learn, you will naturally become very knowledgeable very quickly about your subject. Actually wanting to learn is the essence of becoming an expert and it will also increase your enjoyment during the learning process.

The value of silver is a difficult question, especially, after all, as an object is only worth what someone is prepared to pay for it at any particular point in time. The more important aspects to grasp about collecting are the rarity, quality, condition, and desirability of an item, which are all central factors as to the likely value of a piece.

It is better to develop a good knowledge and a keen eye than to be fixated with values. It is extremely important to handle and look properly at a piece you intend to buy. Just because a silver porringer dates from the reign of Charles II, it does not mean that it is automatically valuable, even though the person selling it to you may insist it is. Do not only look at the hallmark. What about the color of the metal? Is it worn? Are there any holes in the object or has it been repaired? Is it wearing thin on the sides? Is the piece in fact in such poor condition that it is now beyond redemption? After all, it may be old but it is only a silver drinking cup, of which thousands may have been made.

Hopefully a carefully built-up collection will not only be a joy to own but also a valuable nest egg, particularly over the passage of 15 years or more – short-term investment potential is more risky. So be patient and enjoy collecting and all the pleasure and excitement that goes with it.

ALEXIS BUTCHER

The values given in this book for featured objects reflect the sort of prices you might expect to pay for similar pieces at an auction house or from a dealer. As there are so many variable factors involved in the pricing of antiques, such as the condition of the item, where you purchase it, and market trends, the values given should be used as a general guide only.

PERIODS & STYLES

BAROQUE	QUEEN ANNE OR EARLY GEORGIAN

- **Period** 17thC–early 18thC
- **Characteristics** heavy, grand forms; bold, bulbous shapes; abundant ornamentation; elaborate carving; rich gilding
- **Motifs** acanthus; fruit and flowers; pediments; caryatids; putti; cornucopia; eagles; trophies; swags; lion's paw feet
- **Important monarchs** Louis XI; Charles II; William and Mary

- **Period** 1702–1714 (reign of Queen Anne); c.1714–c.1727 (Early Georgian)
- **Characteristics** restraint; minimal decoration; architectural style
- **Motifs** coats-of-arms, crests and armorials; masks; acanthus; architectural mouldings; eagles; trophies; swags; lion's paw feet
- **Key silversmiths** Paul de Lamerie; Philip Rollos; Anthony Nelme; Benjamin Pyne

ROCOCO	FEDERAL

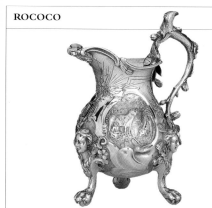

- **Period** early to mid-18thC
- **Characteristics** light, playful, rustic scenes; curved, organic forms; asymmetry; light gilding; pale woods; pastel colors
- **Motifs** flamboyant scrollwork; flowers and foliage; shells; rocaille (rockwork); scrolls; ribbons; flutes; grotesques; chinoiseries
- **Key silversmiths** Paul de Lamerie; Paul Crespin
- **Important monarchs** George II; Louis XV

- **Period** c.1789–1830
- **Characteristics** the Federal style is the later North American version of the Neo-classical style of the mid- to late 18thC; forms from Classical antiquity; symmetry
- **Motifs** beading, reeding and fluting; vase and urn shapes; guilloche; gadrooning; Greek key; palmettes; acanthus; husks; trophies; griffins; anthemion; wreaths
- **Key silversmiths** Paul Revere

VICTORIAN

- **Period** 1837–1901
- **Characteristics** revivals of historical styles; emphasis on heavy, ponderous decoration; extravagant ornament and showiness; mass-production; novelty designs
- **Motifs** motifs and elements from different periods randomly combined (eclecticism)
- **Key silversmiths** Elkington & Co.; Messrs Fox; William Comyns; Hamilton & Inches

ART NOUVEAU

- **Period** 1890s–c.1915
- **Characteristics** sinuous, organic, asymmetrical forms; curving lines; stylized naturalism; asymmetry; symbolism
- **Motifs** whiplash curves; plants, flowers, leaves; dragonflies, scarabs butterflies; women with long flowing hair and diaphanous gowns
- **Key silversmiths** Tiffany & Co.; Liberty & Co.; Omar Ramsden

ART DECO

- **Period** c.1918–1940
- **Characteristics** streamlined, geometric, stylized forms based on machines, abstract art and architecture; elements derived from African and Egyptian art
- **Motifs** fashionable women; chevrons; zigzags; squares; circles; triangles; sunbursts; lightning bolts; abstract geometric patterns
- **Key silversmiths** J.-E. Puiforcat; Christofle; Georg Jensen; Gorham Manufacturing Co.

MODERN

- **Period** post c.1945
- **Characteristics** organic, biomorphic, asymmetrical shapes; sculptural forms; functionalism; mass-production
- **Motifs** abstract themes derived from the scientific world; bold architectural designs and organic motifs
- **Key silversmiths** Stuart Devlin; Alessi; Robert Welch; Gerald Benney; Sigurd Persson

PART 1

BUYING & SELLING

SILVER

ABOVE A 19THC TEA SERVICE, $640–960.

LEFT A SELECTION OF SILVER FROM CHRISTIE'S
SOUTH KENSINGTON, LONDON.

STARTING A COLLECTION

Although few people are fortunate enough to inherit a collection of valuable silver, many will have acquired a silver christening mug, napkin ring, spoon, vase, or teapot – pieces that traditionally mark rites of passage and spark an interest in finding out more about how and where they were made.

Collectors of silver are very fortunate, as the object of their passion has a long, well-documented history; it encompasses all the major decorative art styles; it is available in quantity, internationally, and in a huge variety of styles and forms. Where you start will depend on two major factors: first and foremost, what appeals to you; and, second, what you can afford. Other points to bear in mind are how much space you have available in which to display your collection, and how much time you can devote to collecting and cleaning. Even if space and time are limited, the choice is vast. Some collectors concentrate on a particular period or

decorative style such as Rococo, Neo-classical, Georgian, Regency, Victorian, or Art Nouveau. Others collect silver from a specific country or by a well-known maker, or prefer items of local interest or commemorative pieces. Some collectors concentrate on particular items, for example, teapots, coffeepots, candlesticks, or, a favorite among novices, small, modestly priced, readily available objects such as caddy spoons, wine labels, vesta cases, card cases, or spoons. Some collections consist of more unusual novelty items, for example pap boats, stirrup cups, rattles, or wine funnels. For those who are simply bowled over by the timeless appeal of the soft gleaming luster of a precious metal that has been used to make domestic, religious, and decorative items since ancient times, it may just be a case of love at first sight.

A visit to a good museum is an invaluable source of both inspiration and information, even if you have already decided on a particular collecting area. Looking around well-documented displays will give you a good

> **COLLECTOR'S CHECKLIST**
> - BUY WHAT YOU LIKE
> - BUY THE BEST YOU CAN
> - LEARN ABOUT SILVER FROM BOOKS AND MUSEUMS
> - GAIN EXPERIENCE OF HANDLING SILVER BY VISITING AUCTION HOUSES, FAIRS, AND ANTIQUES SHOPS

A magnifying glass, tape measure, knife, brush (for cleaning dirty hallmarks), and books on collecting and marks are useful tools for new collectors.

Small items such as cigarette cases are a good place to start as they are easy to house and can be very affordable.

visual guide to periods, styles, and well-known makers, as well as an idea of the vast range of shapes and forms available. There are numerous authoritative guides on all aspects of silver (*see* p.168), which are another valuable source of background information, available in libraries. Once you have done your homework – or, better still, as you are doing it – try to gain experience of actually handling silver, because careful handling and close inspection is the only way to build up the practical experience that is the basis of all expertise. Visit fairs, markets, auction previews – any place where you are able to pick up silver, handle it, look at it, and gradually become accustomed to the feel of it – while learning about prices and availability.

Armed with this basic knowledge you can begin to buy. Visit specialist dealers' shops, auctions, markets, fairs, jumble, and car-boot sales – the wider the range of venues the better, as that will help you to get some idea of the best and most profitable sources of the pieces you want to collect.

Always buy the very best you can afford. Good quality and pristine condition do not come cheap, but they do hold their value. A piece that has to be restored may in the long run cost more than a higher-priced piece in better condition and is far less likely to hold its price, let alone appreciate in value. Try to buy silver that is as near to original condition as possible (this is often difficult in the case of domestic silver, but is worth it). Avoid pieces where armorials or initials have been polished out, or which have been repaired or restored.

A friendly specialist dealer – many of whom would happily describe themselves as collectors whose habit got out of control – can be an invaluable asset for a novice collector, guiding you through the quicksands of condition and restoration, although such information and advice will only be forthcoming as a long-term relationship is built up. This is all too likely to happen as – be warned – silver is addictive, and your collection may mushroom.

You should obtain and keep receipts for all your purchases, with details of where and when you bought the piece, from whom, and the price you paid, plus any information about condition and restoration. Not only will such detailed information be helpful for insurance purposes, it will also help you to keep abreast of market trends and see whether your collection is a costly addiction or a profitable pastime. However, not every piece will be an investment. Trends in collecting change, which is why it is crucial to purchase a piece that you like, and, even better, which you can also use, so that you profit in terms of enjoyment if not money. If you follow the basic rule of buying the best you can afford – which applies to all areas of collecting – should you want or have to sell all or part of your collection, you may be surprised at how rewarding collecting silver can be.

At the top of the collecting scale are such fine pieces as this vase (1893) by Tiffany & Co.

AUCTIONS

In spite of apocryphal stories of innocent bystanders buying expensive lots merely by inadvertently scratching an ear at the wrong moment, auction houses remain a major and popular source of silver for both new and experienced collectors. In the saleroom, trade and private buyers can compete on equal terms for both the tiny minority of pieces that make headline-grabbing figures and the vast majority of items that are far more modestly priced. So, if you are inspired by the thrill of the hunt, auctions can provide not only an affordable way of buying silver but also a very exciting environment in which to do so.

The major American auction houses (Christie's and Sotheby's) have regular general silver sales for smaller or more modestly priced pieces, in addition to fine or important silver sales. Sales may be subdivided into date or subject categories such as Antique Silver (pre-1899), Modern Silver (post-1898), or Spoons and Flatware. Items may be included in mixed sales or grouped by date.

The city sales held by the main auction houses tend to be the province of the dealer and the serious private collector, and the quality of the silver (and the prices) reflects this. The regional branches have more general sales, where the pieces and prices tend to be more modest. Other provincial general sales are run by independent auctioneers. You can phone around to check on precise dates and details of sales and ask to be put on a mailing list. Lists of auction houses and auctioneers are available in specialist publications and directories. However prestigious or modest the sale, the golden rule is to prepare carefully, and the following guidelines will help you do just that.

BUYING AT AUCTION CHECKLIST
- **READ THROUGH THE CATALOG CAREFULLY**
- **TAKE YOUR TIME AT THE VIEWING**
- **STICK TO YOUR LIMIT**

CATALOGS

Sale catalogs, which range from the glossy color publications of the large auction houses to the typed sheets of small local auctions, list all the items for sale (known as "lots"), together with their lot numbers, in the order in which they will be sold. In large auction-house catalogs each lot will have a description, including the date it was made, the maker (if known) and details of provenance and any damage or restoration. Auction-house catalogs are bound by the Trade Descriptions Act, and, although most include a disclaimer that they reflect only the "opinion" of the cataloguer, should what was described as an 18thC coffeepot later turn out to be a 19thC reproduction, you will have some recourse. Most catalogs include an estimated price, which is no guarantee of the final outcome – indeed half the excitement of an auction are the surprise highs and lows of the hammer prices.

Attending auctions is an excellent way for novice and expert collectors alike to learn more about silver.

A few of the vast number of items available at auction.

Invest time at the viewing to make a careful inspection of any items that particularly interest you.

VIEWING

A few days before the sale, the lots are put on view to the public. This is your chance to examine the pieces you are interested in. Check them carefully for hallmarks, condition, surface color and any repairs or restoration. Not only will you be able to make sure that the piece lives up to its catalog description but also, through actually handling different pieces of silver, you will be laying the foundations of true expertise. If you want more information about a piece, ask. The specialist in charge may well be able to provide it, and the larger auction houses should provide a condition report free of charge. At small rural auctions, viewing might entail sorting through boxes of household clearance items, and it pays to go armed with patience and optimism.

PAYMENT

The viewing is also a good opportunity to clarify procedures for bidding and payment. Although many smaller auction houses will ask for your name and address only when you have successfully bid for and secured a lot, if you intend to bid at a large sale, you may need to register in advance, or on the day. Usually this entails filling in a form giving details of your name, address and bank account. In return you will be issued with a "paddle" – a card with your bidding number on it. Check whether the auction house accepts credit cards, whether cheques will need to be cleared before goods are released, and if there is a time limit within which goods need to be collected. Most auction houses expect lots to be paid for and collected within five working days, after which you might be charged interest and storage.

ATTENDING THE SALE

Having read through the catalog, been to the viewing to check the lots you are interested in, clarified bidding and payment procedures and decided on your price limit, the next step is to attend the sale and bid. If the lot you want to bid for is towards the end of a long sale, check with a member of staff how quickly the lots are likely to be sold and when you need to arrive. Try to stick to your price limit rather than get carried away in the excitement of the saleroom. Should your bid be successful, the auctioneer will bring down the gavel at that price, and your "paddle" number will be written down in the "auctioneer's book" as a legally binding confirmation of the sale.

If you are unable to attend the sale, the commissions clerk or auctioneer can bid on your behalf. They are duty bound to buy as inexpensively as they can and will follow instructions on maximum bids. They might expect a tip (5 to 10% of the hammer price) if they are successful on your behalf.

BIDDING

The auctioneer announces the lot number of the item to be sold, and bidding usually starts just below the price listed in the catalog. If there are no bids at this price, the auctioneer may lower the price until bidding starts. Buyers can join the bidding at any stage by attracting the auctioneer's attention. Contrary to popular rumour, this may initially prove difficult. However, once you have become part of the bidding the auctioneer will come back to you, and your nod or shake of the head will indicate an acceptance or a refusal of the new price. The price rises in increments of about 10% of the estimated price, although this may vary at the discretion of the auctioneer.

The price at which the gavel falls and the bidding stops is known as the hammer price. In addition to the hammer price, you will be liable for the auction-house premium – between 10 and 15% of the hammer price – plus sales tax on the premium. Read the conditions of sale section of the catalog carefully: a description accompanied by an asterisk or a dagger mark might mean that you will be liable for sales tax on the hammer price and the premium.

Some items have a reserve price to make sure that they are not sold for far less than their value because an auction is poorly attended. Should a lot in which you are particularly interested remain unsold because it did not make its reserve price, it may be worth approaching the auctioneer after the sale to see if the vendor will accept a very near offer.

SELLING

If you decide to sell a piece from your collection through an auction house, bear in mind that auction houses sell on your behalf, rather than buying directly from you as a dealer does. There is usually no charge for an over-the-counter valuation, and you are under no obligation to sell based on this valuation. However, should you decide to sell, you will be charged commission (usually 10 to 15% of the hammer price), sales tax on the commission, an insurance charge, and a handling charge. If your item is illustrated in the catalog you might also be charged a fee to cover photographic costs. The advantages of selling through an auction house are good publicity and the presence of a wide range of potential buyers who may be prepared to pay over the odds for an unusual piece that is new to the market.

Items are marked with their catalog lot numbers, so that they are easy to identify. However, always read catalog descriptions carefully, as lots made up of several items (known as part lots) might not all be displayed together.

ANTIQUES SHOPS, JUNK SHOPS & CHARITY SHOPS

The glamour and excitement of the auction saleroom can be somewhat intimidating for the novice collector, who, along with many more experienced collectors, may find that an antiques dealer is one of the easiest and safest sources of silver, provided that he or she is a member of a recognized trade association.

in the shop (if you are in any doubt ask). It means that the dealer is a member of a professional body; that he or she has been registered and trading for at least three years, has a thorough knowledge of his or her subject and good-quality stock and, above all, adheres to a strict code of fair practice that includes accurate description of stock and clear pricing. Members are vetted on a regular basis to make sure that they maintain the standards that are demanded by the relevant professional bodies.

DEALERS

In the USA there are two main professional bodies for antiques dealers: the National Art & Antiques Dealers' Association (NAADA) and the Art & Antique Dealers League of America (AADLA). In Britain the equivalent bodies are the Association of Art and Antique Dealers (generally known as LAPADA) and the British Antique Dealers' Association (BADA) and and the majority of European countries have similar organizations. Membership of one of these bodies is usually indicated by a NAADA or AADLA logo displayed in the window or

> **BUYING AT DEALERS CHECKLIST**
> - MAKE SURE THAT THE DEALER IS A MEMBER OF A REPUTABLE TRADE BODY
> - TAKE YOUR TIME WHEN DECIDING WHAT TO BUY
> - CHECK WHETHER ANY REPAIRS OR RESTORATION HAVE BEEN CARRIED OUT
> - HAGGLE TO GET THE BEST PRICE POSSIBLE
> - GET A DETAILED RECEIPT

The antiques associations can provide lists of members throughout the country. Members of each organization can then be further divided down into general dealers, who carry a wide range of all types of antiques, and specialist dealers, who concentrate on either a particular period, such as Art Deco and Art Nouveau, or a particular medium, such as silver. As might be expected, specialist dealers usually have more expertise in their particular area than more general dealers.

Antiques dealers are often collectors whose habit has got out of control, and you might be fortunate enough to find one who is willing to share his or her knowledge and enthusiasm with you and build up a longterm relationship that will be mutually beneficial. He or she may be prepared to look out for special pieces for your collection and offer advice on the most modest purchase. A friendly dealer may even be prepared to buy back stock in order tohelp you trade up as your knowledge grows, your tastes change, and you begin to see the advantage of buying one good piece with your monthly budget of, for example, $160, rather than two less-inspiring pieces that cost $80 each.

Dealers are usually only too happy to provide information and advice about their silver for sale.

One of the major advantages of buying from a dealer rather than an auction house is that you can take your time deciding just how much you are prepared to pay for a piece. Always ask dealers – politely – for their "best" price, especially if you are considering buying several items.

Many dealers are happy to consider special payment arrangements for regular customers, and they may even hold a piece for you while you make up your mind. It also pays to find out as much as you can about the item that has caught your eye: ask about condition, restoration, any marks, and any details of the provenance. The other advantage of buying from a dealer is that, once you have made up your mind that you cannot live without a particular piece, you know exactly how much it will cost, as there are none of the "extras" associated with buying at a saleroom such as auction-house premiums or commission for someone bidding on your behalf.

Every purchase should be accompanied by a detailed receipt featuring the dealer's name, trading address, a full description of the piece (name of maker/manufacturer if known, date or approximate date of production, details of any restoration or known damage), and the price paid. These receipts are not only useful as a record of your collection, and for insurance purposes, but will also be needed should there be any later problems or disputes over authenticity. In the unlikely event of such a dispute, ask the antiques associations about conciliation services between customers and registered members of their associations.

Prices may be higher when buying from a dealer, who will put his or her markup on stock, much of which will have been bought at auction. However, even though a piece may therefore cost you more than it would have done if you had successfully bid for it at auction, a regular customer may well be able to negotiate a very competitive price, and/or have the piece on approval. The slightly higher price may also reflect the cost of any cleaning, repair or restoration work carried out at the dealer's expense, and this is

The array of fine silver available through antiques dealers offers endless opportunities for building up a collection.

likely to be significantly lower than you would have had to pay if you had bought the piece on your own behalf at auction.

JUNK SHOPS AND CHARITY SHOPS

You are very unlikely to find an undiscovered valuable treasure in the well-displayed interior of a specialist silver dealer's showroom, but it might be possible to find interesting piece in the less-sophisticated premises of a junk shop or charity shop.

The contents of junk shops are often job-lots from house-clearance sales, many of which have already been scoured by dealers. However, a trawl through dusty boxes (arming yourself with a flashlight and possibly a pair of gloves for those dark, dirty corners) may reveal an undetected potential bargain for which you can haggle and emerge triumphant. Always ask for a receipt, but do not expect it to give the same accurate details of date, maker, repair, style, or condition that you would expect from a reputable dealer, nor will there be any redress should your bargain fail to live up to its description or your expectations. Beware too of descriptions, both verbal and written, that contain the word "style". A coffeepot in the Georgian "style" is not guaranteed to be a genuine piece of Georgian silver; it may well instead be a later reproduction.

Charity shops have an eclectic mix of bric-a-brac that may include an undiscovered bargain, and in general their prices are extremely modest. Prices are usually clearly marked and are not normally susceptible to negotiation. As a rule, any immediately recognizable good pieces – coffeepots, teapots, cream jugs, sugar bowls, spoons – will have been creamed off, but a good grounding in your subject, and a keen eye and a "feel" for silver, can yield pleasant surprises, especially of more unusual or novelty items that are perhaps badly tarnished or not immediately recognizable as silver. However, do not be tempted by readily found pieces in poor condition; these will often cost far more to restore or repair than can ever be justified in terms of selling on or trading up.

SELLING TO A DEALER

If you decide to sell a piece from your collection, make sure that you go to a dealer who specializes not only in silver but also in the particular period or style of the item. An expert on Neo-classical silver may not be the best judge of the value of, for example, an electroplated German Art Nouveau vase. It is sensible to telephone first rather than just turn up at what may be an inconvenient time. Using the lists drawn up by the antiques associations, you can phone around dealers with a detailed description of your piece to see who may be interested in buying it. Send a follow-up

> **SELLING THROUGH DEALERS CHECKLIST**
> - ESTABLISH WHO WOULD BE THE MOST APPROPRIATE DEALER TO SELL TO
> - CONTACT SEVERAL DEALERS TO ENSURE THAT YOU ARE BEING GIVEN INFORMATION THAT IS REPRESENTATIVE
> - CONSIDER SENDING THE DEALER A PHOTOGRAPH OF YOUR ITEM PRIOR TO VISITING HIS OR HER SHOP

photograph if requested and then take the piece along to the dealer's shop; he or she may visit you if you have several pieces to sell.

Check the value of the item with more than one person before agreeing to sell, as opinions may vary, and you do not have the safeguard of the public arena of the saleroom, where in general a piece will realize its market value even if it has been undervalued in the sale catalog. It may also be a sensible idea to take the item you want to sell to one of the auction houses and ask for an over-the-counter valuation, as this can be done without any obligation to sell. One major advantage of selling directly to a dealer is that you know exactly how much you will be paid – there will be no deductions for commission, insurance, sales tax or, possibly, photographic charges. You will

The London Silver Vaults in Chancery Lane is a treasure-trove for anyone interested in silver. Over 40 dealers, all trading exclusively in silver, are based in the Vaults, making this a fascinating place to look at, buy, and sell silver.

Never be afraid to ask a dealer any questions you have over price, date, and the maker or designer, and always check whether or not any restoration or repair has been carried out on the piece.

also receive your money immediately, without having to wait for your piece to be catalogued, entered in the appropriate sale and sold, and with the possible further delay of some weeks before the payment reaches you after the sale.

Selling directly through a dealer also ensures that you avoid the disappointment of your piece failing to reach its reserve price at auction, which in turn will make it much more difficult to sell to a dealer. Antiques dealers may often be reluctant to take pieces that have not managed to sell in the saleroom and are therefore no longer considered "fresh" to the market. Should you be selling to a dealer with whom you have built up a good longterm relationship, you may be able to

trade in a piece in order then to be able to trade up and buy a more valuable piece, which would then be to your and the dealer's mutual advantage.

"KNOCKERS"

Never be tempted to sell to "knockers" – people who make unsolicited calls to your home or put leaflets through the door offering to buy unwanted furniture or bric-a-brac. Many knockers are unscrupulous, disreputable operators who try to trick the elderly and vulnerable into parting with their property for much less than it is actually worth. There is also the added risk of allowing into your home an unknown person, who may be using the visit as an opportunity to plan to return later without an invitation. It is also very inadvisable to advertise silver for sale in periodicals, as this may encourage unwanted interest in your collection.

FAIRS, MARKETS & BOOT SALES

As the interest in antiques has grown, so too has the number of antiques fairs of all descriptions, from major international and national affairs to smaller-scale local ones. Many dealers are now considering abandoning their expensive retail premises in favor of private sales or regular stands at the many large, prestigious antiques fairs that attract collectors from all over the world.

MAJOR FAIRS

Major fairs give new collectors the chance to see a number of specialist silver dealers' stalls under one roof, establish a picture of the huge range of pieces and styles that are available, and generally compare prices and stock. Fairs also provide an opportunity for dealers from far-flung places to make contact with potential new clients, and for novice collectors to examine the stock of dealers with whom they might otherwise never have occasion to come into contact without traveling long distances.

The lively atmosphere at fairs makes them a great day out for lovers of antiques.

Major international and national fairs are advertised in the press, specialist publications and antiques shops, and if you have a good relationship with a particular dealer, he or she might send you details or even an invitation. As a general visitor you will probably have to pay to get into one of these fairs, which are usually held in large prestigious venues (see pp.166–7), but remember that you will be saving considerably on travel costs and time by seeing a wide range of dealers from all parts of the country, and possibly the globe, under one roof. The entrance fee may well include a catalog listing all the exhibitors, together with their addresses, telephone numbers, and, where relevant, fax and e-mail details. These catalogs are invaluable reference material for collectors. It is also worth chatting to dealers to find out what other stock they hold, and perhaps arranging to contact them after the fair or asking to be advised about which other fairs they will be attending.

For many dealers, these fairs are an opportunity to see and be seen by fellow dealers as well as potential buyers. Some put on wonderful displays, perhaps including extra-special pieces to dazzle and outshine the opposition, so do not assume that all their stock is necessarily outside your price range. Fairs give dealers a chance to make contact with potential new customers whose budgets vary widely, so take the opportunity to ask questions and find out whether their stock includes items that are within your price range, and whether their particular passion coincides with yours.

The quality of the stock, and the prices, reflect the status of the exhibitors and the fair, so such events are rarely a place for bargains. What they offer the novice collector is a good chance to see a range of the very best pieces

---

BUYING AT FAIRS, MARKETS & BOOT SALES CHECKLIST

- GET THERE EARLY TO FIND THE BEST BARGAINS
- COMPARE PRICES AT DIFFERENT STALLS
- TAKE CASH WITH YOU IF YOU INTEND TO BUY
- TRY TO GET A RECEIPT

available outside the auction houses and possibly to make contact with a non-local dealer whose stock and specialist knowledge of a particular collecting area may make a longer journey worthwhile. Items bought at major fairs can usually be paid for with credit cards or travelers' cheques. A proper detailed, fully descriptive receipt for each item should be provided as a matter of course.

"VETTED" FAIRS

"Vetted" fairs are made up of invited stall holders, specially chosen for their expertise, their reputations and the quality of their stock. All pieces in the show are "vetted" by independent experts in the field, who check carefully for authenticity, condition, over-restoration, and accuracy of descriptions. Items displayed at "date-line" fairs are vetted for accuracy of dating to ensure, for example, that a piece of silver that appears in an Art Deco fair was in fact made in the 1920s or 1930s and is not a 1950s copy, and that all the items for sale in a fair devoted to pre-1900 silver were indeed made prior to the turn of the century.

Although prices at vetted fairs reflect the extra administration costs that are associated with such meticulous

Arrive early to pick up the best pieces such as this matching teapot, milk jug, and sugar bowl (1878).

assessment, novice collectors can enjoy peace of mind and make use of a superb training ground in which to become familiar with the elusive feel and look of a particular period or style that will enable you to buy more confidently at less scrupulously monitored events. As at all large fairs, credit cards, and travelers' cheques should usually be accepted, and there should be no problems about the authenticity of items.

SMALLER FAIRS

Numerous smaller antiques fairs also take place throughout the country, often timed to coincide with peak visitor and tourist months. Your entrance fee will be far more modest than that charged for the major or vetted fairs, but the exhibitors will probably have less expertise, and their stock will not have been vetted, so you will have to rely much more on your own judgement as to dating, restoration, and authencity. On the plus side, you may be lucky enough to find a bargain, but make sure that you get a proper receipt including details of the vendor, his or her address, a description of the piece, and the price you paid for it. Another advantage is that the stock will usually be more modestly priced. Should you decide to splash out, many (although not all) dealers accept credit cards or cheques with a banker's card; however, cash may prove to be a better alternative, as some dealers offer a modest discount for a cash sale.

MARKETS

The majority of capital cities have antiques markets that are big attractions for both tourists and collectors alike. Details of where and when these markets take place are generally available from tourist information offices or in guide books.

In London, the Portobello Road, Camden Passage, Grays Antique Market, and Alfies Antiques Market are on most collectors' visiting list; in Paris, antiques lovers can try the Marché aux Puces. Some markets have permanent stalls and are open almost every day (if possible, phone beforehand to check); others operate on only one or two days a week. You will need to arrive early for the latter, armed with a flashlight and a large dose of common sense. Such markets are often used as a way of disposing of stolen goods or fakes, so get a detailed written receipt if you can, or at least make a note of where and when you made your purchase and how much you paid for it. You will have no recourse if your bargain turns out to be a fake, but should an item turn out to have been stolen, a receipt will prove that you bought it in good faith. To be absolutely certain of securing your piece, take cash, but, especially if you are abroad, keep it in a secure place, and familiarize yourself with the currency beforehand to avoid the problem of having to change large denomination notes.

BUYING AT BOOT SALES & FLEA MARKETS

Car-boot sales and flea markets are now a regular feature of town and country life. They are held in farmers' fields, school playgrounds, car parks, disused airfields, or church or school halls, and so on, often on a regular basis. Advertisements appear in the local press and shops, or even just pinned to streetlights or trees. Although dealers are often first on the scene, it is possible to find interesting pieces among the bric-a-brac of attic and shed clearances. Many amateur dealers operate at car-boot sales, so examine pieces carefully for damage and restoration; always use your own judgement as to date and authenticity.

Prices are negotiable, but you are most unlikely to get a receipt for any purchase, so it is a good idea to try to make a note of where and when you bought the piece, possibly jotting down the registration number of the car if it was at a car-boot sale. Bear in mind that these are fertile areas for stolen goods and, occasionally, counterfeit notes, so make sure that you have plenty of smaller denomination notes to avoid the risk of being given large denomination notes as change. Sales can also be a fertile ground for pickpockets, who know that buyers will be carrying money in cash and more preoccupied with bargain hunting than checking on who is behind them. Buyers and sellers are advised to keep any cash secure in a money belt.

This is just one of the many stalls at Camden Passage in London's Islington – a favorite haunt of antiques collectors.

SELLING AT BOOT SALES

Boot sales are ideal places to dispose of those embarrassing impulse buys, or pieces you have "outgrown" but would not interest a dealer. Try to arrive early to make sure you get a good position and are set up and organized before the rush begins. Dealers usually arrive first and descend en masse on a new car to cast a jaundiced and an experienced eye over your goods. Have an idea of the price you want, and do not be bullied into parting with anything unless you feel it is fair.

Be prepared to bargain, and do not be surprised to see a piece you sold earlier being displayed at another stall at twice the price. Boot sales are normally cash only, so make sure you have plenty of change so that you are not persuaded to sell at a lower price because you cannot provide change from a large note. Security is important – as a seller, make sure your front car doors are locked while you do business from the back of the car. The risk of being given faked notes means that it is wise to deal in small denomination notes only.

Fairs and boot sales may be the place to pick up a bargain.

PART 2

CARE & SECURITY

ABOVE A CADDY SHOVEL BY JOSEPH TAYLOR OF
BIRMINGHAM, 1815, $320–400.

LEFT ONE OF THE MANY WAYS OF DISPLAYING
YOUR SILVER COLLECTION.

CARE & RESTORATION

Silver is a durable metal, and silver objects in good condition require little care other than occasional cleaning and polishing to prevent the build-up of tarnish. However, it is likely that some pieces may be damaged by rough handling or use. Die-stamped wares made from the late 18thC – common on the market today – are made of very thin-gauge metal, which can break, split or crack. Such defects can easily be repaired by an expert silversmith, but you should never to try to restore or repair damaged silver at home. This is because the restoration of silver, unlike that of items in other materials, may have legal implications. Even the application of a small feature such as a missing finial, or of patches to repair splits where handles have pulled away from the body, could constitute an addition rather than a repair, and the object may need to be reassayed and then remarked, especially if it is to be resold.

> **CARE & RESTORATION CHECKLIST**
> - ALWAYS USE A PROFESSIONAL RESTORER FOR REPAIRS
> - EXERCISE GREAT CAUTION WHEN CLEANING SILVER
> - STORE ITEMS CAREFULLY

One of the most important aspects of keeping silver clean is the prevention of tarnish. Silver will develop black marks in contact with sulphur, found in the air, especially in polluted city atmospheres, or in fumes from burning oil and gas. Sulphur is also found in foods such as eggs, peas, and brussels sprouts. Both hydrogen sulphide, which is found in emulsion paint, household fabrics, and flooring, and ammonia will also discolour silver. If you acquire heavily tarnished silver – perhaps through inheritance, for example – always take expert advice, as the tarnish is extremely difficult to remove. When the tarnish is removed, some of the silver surface will be also be deposited on the cleaning cloth as silver sulphide.

CLEANING

If an object is not heavily tarnished, clean it after buying or acquiring it with a proprietary cleaner or wadding polish. Some modern proprietary cleaners contain tarnish inhibitors that will help to keep the silver in pristine condition over a long period. Never use an abrasive cleaner – in the past, jeweler's rouge (calcined ferrous sulphate) was used, with the result that many 18th and 19thC pieces available today are scratched and have a hard, brilliant shine rather than a characteristic warm luster. After the first cleaning the silver can be kept in good condition by regular washing with warm, soapy water (using a mild detergent), rinsing, and drying with a soft cotton or chamois cloth. In this way the silver will develop a soft, glowing lustre, called a "skin" or "patina". Silver-gilt and plated wares can be treated in the same way, but care must be taken when washing and drying silver-gilt objects, for example snuff boxes, with delicate decoration such as filigree and enamel. Silver should be rubbed over occasionally to prevent the build-up of tarnish, but too frequent rubbing or polishing will destroy the patina and wear away

Early American silver is extremely rare, and this 18thC coffeepot is still very valuable in spite of its poor condition.

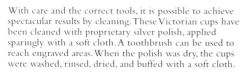

With care and the correct tools, it is possible to achieve spectacular results by cleaning. These Victorian cups have been cleaned with proprietary silver polish, applied sparingly with a soft cloth. A toothbrush can be used to reach engraved areas. When the polish was dry, the cups were washed, rinsed, dried, and buffed with a soft cloth.

both the marks and bright-cut, engraved, or flat-chased details. Similarly, overzealous polishing of plated wares will wear away the thin layer of silver plate, and cause the copper base to show through. Particular care should be taken when cleaning and polishing plated wares with protruding features such as scroll feet, which are especially vulnerable to wear.

Silver dips may be effective for larger items such as tureens, and for cleaning objects with complex shapes or decoration. However, they must be used with care and only sparingly: always use a non-metallic bath, and do not leave the objects in the dip for too long, as the chemicals may begin to attack the surface of the silver, turning it dull and matte.

Pierced silver, especially pieces made of thin-gauge metal from the late 18thC, should be handled and cleaned carefully as the piercing may split. Do not clean pierced work with a cloth as the fabric may catch in the edges. Instead, use a very fine soft brush and soapy water. This method is also good for removing the remains of jeweler's rouge or other abrasive cleaning powders from older pieces. Use a weak solution of washing soda and water to clean heavily stained teapots and coffeepots. Many candlesticks dating from the last 150

years are filled in the base ("loaded") with tar, plaster of Paris or resin for stability, as they were made of very thin rolled sheet metal rather than being cast. Do not immerse these in very hot water, or leave them exposed in direct sunlight on a table or mantelpiece, as the tar or resin will expand under heat, pushing off the base. Knife handles are also sometimes loaded – similarly, do not clean these in very hot water or put them in the dishwasher, as the loading in the handle will expand, pushing off the blade. Particular care must be taken with ivory or mother-of-pearl handles on knives, forks, and

If an item is as badly damaged as this bent and creased tazza (1920) always seek the advice of an expert.

other flatware that have a steel tang (shaft) running down the center, joining the handle with the blade. These should not be put in water as the steel will rust, and the tang will swell and split the handles.

STORAGE AND HANDLING

Store silver in clean, dry, airtight cupboards or drawers or in a strong box to keep it in fine condition. To prevent scratches and dents make sure that several pieces stored or displayed together do not touch: thin rim wires, found on jugs, sauceboats, wine coolers, and other dining silver, tend to be particularly subject to denting. Objects with a high content of pure silver – for example, items made in Britannia standard silver, which is 95.8% pure silver – will be softer and scratch more easily than those with a lower content of pure silver; this is also applicable to the pure silver employed on items that are electroplated. Storage in an airtight place is vital, as dampness encourages tarnish to develop; it is also harmful to wooden handles and finials, on such items as teapots, that can rot and crack with changes in temperature and humidity. You should wrap objects, even such small items as flatware, separately in acid-free tissue paper and put them inside a polythene bag, making sure that the polythene does not touch the silver; expel air from the bag and tie it securely. This will maintain pieces in pristine condition for many years. If silver is supplied with its original case (rare), it is usually best to store the piece inside it, although wooden cases may give off acetic acid that will damage the silver. Consult an expert if in doubt.

Salt is very harmful to silver, "burning" into the surface and leaving black spots that are almost impossible to remove. Always empty salt from salt cellars, and clean and dry flatware and plates that have come into contact with salt carefully. Avoid storing silver near salt as the salt will permeate the atmosphere and form a deposit on the silver surface. Many household items contain acid, which will leave black marks: the acid in newspaper print, for example, will etch the silver surface, as will rubber bands. When removing wax from candlesticks, do not use a knife or other sharp implement, as this will scratch the surface.

When you are handling silver it is preferable to wear a pair of soft cotton gloves, but otherwise always rub over the surface after handling or the acid sweat in your fingerprints will attack the silver surface. Never lift such items as teapots, coffeepots, vinaigrettes, or snuff boxes by the lid, as hinges are likely to break easily. Similarly, when cleaning and polishing silver, hold the piece firmly by the body or support it on a steady surface, so that the metal does not take the pressure on delicate parts; the feet of jugs, sauceboats, and salvers, for example, can easily be pushed up into the body if pressure is applied too heavily. Handles, especially the delicate loop handles on Neo-classical silver, can pull away from bodies, which causes splits and cracks. Special care should be taken when handling intricate pierced and filigree work.

On this old Sheffield plate wine cooler (c.1820) the copper base is showing through owing to overpolishing, and the rim is dented.

RESTORATION

As a general rule, when buying items for your collection, and especially when buying for investment, try to avoid restored silver, as this will always be less desirable than a piece in pristine condition. However, this is not always practicable, as pieces in their original condition are rare. Always ask for condition reports when buying pieces at auction, and handle items when viewing before a sale, as this will enable you to detect splits, cracks and dents. Any repair will reduce the value of silver, unless the piece is rare or by a top silversmith.

Repairs should always be given to a specialist silversmith, particularly to one who specializes in the subject of your collection, for example caddy spoons. However, expert silversmiths are hard to find, and it is best to contact one through word of mouth or through a recommendation from a reputable dealer or an auction house. Dealers who have a policy of after-sales attention may be able to have your pieces restored or repaired without your having to find a silversmith directly.

If you initially ask a silversmith to undertake minor repairs, this will enable you to find out if he or she is reliable, what prices he or she charges and what type of work he or she specializes in. If you are having pieces restored, it is important that your idea of sympathetic restoration coincides with that of the silversmith. A silversmith should also be able to replate or regild damaged plated or silver-gilt wares. However, it is often difficult to match the original color of the gilding – mercury-gilded objects that were made before c.1840 have a warmer, richer color that the hard, brassy appearance of modern electrogilded pieces – and if a damaged electroplated piece is replated it will cease to look its age. Never attempt to restore silver yourself, especially by using solder, as this may cause irreparable damage and may also be illegal. According to the British 1973 Hallmarking

If silver plate is polished too much, the base copper may show through as on this late Victorian covered tureen.

Act, if the weight of a piece of silver increases by more than six grams subsequent to its original manufacture, the object must be reassayed and remarked before it can be legally sold. Such an increase in weight is deemed to be an "addition" and not a "repair" by the Antique Plate Committee of the Worshipful Company of Goldsmiths, which examines suspect items and attempts to identify fakes and illegal alterations. The use of silver solder for repairs may also be recognized as the introduction of base metal, as it is of a lower standard than sterling silver.

It is often difficult to decide whether you should have pieces remarked if you do not intend to sell them: for example, there is a difference between an original finial on a teapot that has been knocked and repaired, and a piece with a finial made specifically because the original was missing. It is costly to send repaired objects to the assay office for remarking, and new marks will easily be detected by an expert and the price of the piece decreased accordingly.

It may be a beneficial for the silver collector to undertake a basic silversmithing course, offered by art colleges, as this will enable him or her to acquire a knowledge of defects that can and cannot be repaired easily. A greater understanding of silversmithing techniques may also lead to fewer errors in buying damaged pieces of silver.

Practical items such as this candlestick (1825) have often been subjected to excessive polishing, and the decoration may have lost its detail.

DISPLAY

Silver objects are an immediate enhancement to any room, and the reflective gleam and soft luster of silver are shown off particularly well in soft light, especially in candlelight, rather than in the harsh and even light of electricity. When you are considering how to display your silver collection, you should choose a practical method that is most appropriate to your lifestyle and daily routine. If you regularly use your dining or living room as a workspace, for example, it may prove impractical to position a cumbersome dining service on a central table that is also used as a desk. It is also very important to consider security if your silver is visible to passers-by or onlookers, because silver objects are highly attractive to potential burglars.

> ## DISPLAYING YOUR SILVER CHECKLIST
> - CHOOSE A METHOD OF DISPLAY THAT IS APPROPRIATE TO YOUR HOME AND LIFESTYLE AS WELL AS YOUR SILVER
> - AVOID DISPLAYING YOUR COLLECTION IN A WAY THAT WILL ATTRACT UNWANTED ATTENTION

CABINETS

There are two main options when you are deciding how to display your silver collection: whether to display it in cabinets or to show it exposed on view. The advantage of putting silver in cabinets is that it will tarnish less quickly than silver exposed to fumes in the atmosphere, especially in polluted city air.

The best way of acquiring an antique cabinet is to buy one from a reputable antiques dealer, from an auction house or from an old shop display. Sometimes it is useful to have shelves, partitions, and other features of the cabinet altered, to make them more suitable for the requirements of your collecting. It is also a good idea to add draughtproof strips around the edges of the front and back doors of an old cabinet; this should make the cabinet airtight, and prevent the silver from tarnishing as quickly as it might if unprotected from the air.

The type of cabinet used depends on the type and style of objects in your collection. It is also important to consider whether you want to admire the pieces all the time, as might be the case with thimbles, for example, or look at and handle them only occasionally, as in the case of spoons and other flatware. Multi-drawer collectors' cabinets, or "Wellington" chests, are ideal for small items such as snuff boxes, spoons, and vinaigrettes – the drawers of this type of furniture are also usually airtight enough to prevent tarnishing. Narrow, wall-mounted glazed cabinets are especially suitable for housing miniature silver furniture or thimbles and will take up relatively little space in a small room. Also very useful for displaying small items of silver, especially wine labels and spoons that can be viewed from above, are glass-topped specimen tables. Larger objects such as tea and coffee services and dining silver may be displayed attractively in a large freestanding cabinet with

Displaying silver in the context for which it was intended shows a collection to best advantage.

a glazed front, while canteens of flatware can be kept in fitted boxes, or in fitted side tables with drawers. Silver may be seen to greater advantage in top- or side-lit purpose-built or fitted cabinets, especially in alcoves.

TABLES, SIDEBOARDS, AND MANTELPIECES

If you intend to use the silver in your collection, there is nothing better than putting it in a setting appropriate to its use. For example a dressing-table set can be arranged on a dressing table, a centerpiece, or tureen and candlesticks can be placed on a dining table, or wine coasters and wine coolers set on a sideboard. A symmetrical arrangement of elegant candlesticks on either side of a mantelpiece will add balance to an overall room display. Inspiration for such types of display can be gained from antiques collectors' magazines, displays in dealers' shops or auction rooms, or from museum settings. Books of etiquette showing traditional ways of placing dining silver on a table may also provide ideas.

PROTECTION

Items of silver that are exposed to the air will tarnish faster than those kept in airtight cupboards. Unprotected items are also at a greater risk of damage, such as scratches and dents, through incorrect handling than those that are stored away under lock and key. If you have children or pets, make sure you keep silver objects with delicate or sharp-edged pierced work safely out of reach. Never place silver near central heating or any other direct source of heat – with changes in temperature the metal will expand and contract, and such features as hinges on boxes may come loose as a result. Loaded silver candlesticks are also particularly vulnerable to damage when exposed to heat, for example if they are left in strong direct sunlight on a

Silver is not uniquely collected by lovers of traditional-style antiques, as this collection of elegantly displayed minimalist objects exemplifies.

dining table, because the loading, which is made of tar or resin, will expand and push out and distort the base of the candlestick. The regular exposure of silver objects to cigarette smoke will also speed up the accumulation of tarnish, while putting fruit in an épergne or basket may also damage the silver as the acid in fruit may etch the surface and leave black marks. When displaying silver on antique items of furniture, make sure that the silver does not scratch or dent the wood by placing the silver on protective mats if necessary.

> ### PROTECTING YOUR SILVER CHECKLIST
> - KEEP SILVER IN A CABINET TO MINIMIZE TARNISHING
> - STORE YOUR SILVER AWAY FROM SUCH POTENTIAL HAZARDS AS CHILDREN, PETS, AND EXCESS HEAT

SECURITY

Security is one of the most important aspects to consider when building up a collection of silver, because silver objects have traditionally been among the most attractive items to potential burglars. However, today the value of silver is often overestimated: until the early 20thC a coin contained almost its value in silver, but the metal is now less expensive in real terms than at any time in history – the price of melt silver is approximately $4.80 per oz. Nevertheless, small items of silver are especially popular with collectors, and those that are light and portable, such as spoons, boxes, thimbles, nutmeg graters, salt-cellars, and mustard pots, should always be adequately insured.

EXERCISING DISCRETION

The popular idea that silver represents a great store of wealth endures, so it is essential to be discreet when buying and displaying your collection. If you buy from a dealer, you can ask him or her to keep your identity confidential; similarly, if you want to buy at auction but remain anonymous, you can ask

the staff to bid on your behalf. The fewer the number of people who know you have a collection, the smaller the risk of theft. You can also avoid putting temptation in people's way when displaying your collection. If you live in a row house with no curtains, or if your rooms can be overlooked, do not, for example, put a pair of silver candlesticks in the window. It is also important to be as security conscious with plated wares as with sterling silver, because to the untrained eye there is often no obvious difference between the two. If it is difficult to conceal silver from passers-by, you should take sensible precautions regarding the security of your home. A crime prevention officer from your local police station will be able to provide advice on locks, alarms, and other necessary security equipment.

KEEPING YOUR SILVER SAFE CHECKLIST
- DISPLAY YOUR SILVER WITH CARE
- MAKE SURE THAT YOUR COLLECTION IS INSURED TO AN APPROPRIATE VALUE
- KEEP FULL UP-TO-DATE RECORDS IN CASE OF THEFT

VALUATION AND INSURANCE

The increased risk of theft and burglary makes it important to have a collection properly valued and insured. However, the cost of valuation and insurance will depend on the type and purpose of your collection. If you have a collection of small, portable items intended purely for investment and do not want to display them, the objects could be stored in a safety-deposit box in a bank for a nominal insurance fee. However, check whether these fees increase annually, as the cost may outweigh the value of the collection. If you suffer the theft of inherited items that have sentimental value, there may be no point in replacing them and paying large premiums. Silver that is used regularly, for example a collection of flatware for dinner parties, should be adequately insured up to full retail replacement value, because if stolen it is likely that you would buy another set. You may wish to replace stolen or missing items

Such a valuable item as this elaborate "Ice" bowl (1871) by Gorham Manufacturing Co., which features chased-and-applied "icicles", should be well insured against theft.

Auction-house specialists will be happy to spend time evaluating items you are interested in selling.

secondhand at auction, but the level at which you set the insurance value should be discussed with the insurance company and the firm that carries out the valuation. Insuring small items such as boxes, dressing-table silver, and spoons may be surprisingly expensive, because they are light and portable and so incur a higher risk of theft.

Make sure you communicate clearly with your insurance company when insuring your collection, and follow its stipulations, or you may be unable to replace your property in the event of a loss. Check whether items below a certain value are exempt from being noted on an official inventory and whether the insurance company requires an official written valuation.

To obtain a written valuation, contact an auction house or a reputable dealer who specializes in your type of collection. A specialist will be familiar with current prices for the particular type of object or maker in question, and, if your items go missing, he or she would be qualified to help you retrace them if possible, or supply you with similar items should you wish to carry on collecting. An auction house will charge a fee for a written valuation, and as costs vary you should find out about them beforehand. A minimum daily charge may be made – in which case it could be worth taking

in your entire collection at one visit – or a price may be calculated as a percentage of the overall value of the collection. A written valuation should include a full description of each item, with its dimensions and value for insurance purposes; this should be updated every three to four years, as market values fluctuate.

KEEPING A RECORD OF YOUR COLLECTION

The best guarantee of being able to retrace any stolen property is to provide the police with up-to-date, detailed, and accurate records. Keep an inventory of your collection, with careful records of the date you purchased each item, where you bought it and from whom, the price, and whether you paid by cash or cheque. Also note its height, weight, diameter, materials, and decorative features, and give the item an index number in your inventory, known only to you. Marker pens visible under ultraviolet light are also a useful method of recording your details on each piece, though these should be used with great care – consult an expert if in doubt. Make a careful note of any marks, but most importantly, if there is an engraved inscription, crest or coat-of-arms, copy the words or motto out in full, draw it, or take a rubbing of it. Few pieces available on the market today are unique, and the only way of recording a certain item as being yours is to note defects, repairs, decorative features, or inscriptions individual to that piece.

It is useful to take a photograph of each piece in your collection in natural light against a plain background; take close-up shots of any distinctive inscriptions or decoration, scratches, dents, or repairs. Keep one set of photographs with your inventory and at least one other in a secure place such as a bank.

It is possible to trace missing items by contacting the Art Loss Register, a database of stolen property in Britain, or through an advertisement in specialist publications such as the Antiques Trade Gazette or Trace; circulating photocopies of your records and photographs to dealers who trade in the type of items in your collection may also be useful in finding lost pieces.

PART 3

THE BASICS

ABOVE A ROCOCO BASKET WITH LATTICEWORK SIDES
AND A CAST BORDER AND HANDLE,
BY PAUL DE LAMERIE, *C.*1740, $80,000–112,000.

LEFT A DETAIL OF A LATE 19THC TEAPOT,
SHOWING PROFUSE DECORATION OF FLOWERS
AND FOLIAGE, $640–960.

THE METALS

Silver has been treasured throughout history for its rarity, reflective properties and incomparable luminescence. Over the centuries it has been used to create symbols for religious and ceremonial purposes, to mint coinage and to make practical items for the household, as well as precious objects reflecting wealth and status.

Silver's intrinsic value as bullion has proved an important resource during times of economic hardship and political instability, and it has often been melted down and converted into coinage. Silver objects were frequently refashioned to accommodate changing styles and tastes. In the 16thC the conquest of the Americas by the Spanish and the subsequent discovery of vast silver deposits there led to a surge in production as silver was imported in enormous quantities into Europe.

Too soft to be made into wrought objects, pure silver must be alloyed with small amounts of other metals to make it harder and more durable. In the mid-18thC production was revolutionized by fusing silver with copper to produce Sheffield plate, but the introduction of electroplating in the 1840s caused the rapid decline of the Sheffield plate industry.

SILVER STANDARDS

The sterling standard – 92.5% pure silver – has been the legal standard for silver in Britain since the 14thC. A shortage of silver in the late 17thC led to the raising of the standard to 95.8% from 1697 to 1720 in order to discourage the melting down of coinage to produce silver objects. The higher standard was known as the Britannia standard. Silver made in the Britannia standard period is brighter in colour than sterling silver and of a higher quality. The hallmarks were changed to signify that this new standard was in effect. The sterling lion was replaced by the figure of

A Britannia standard serving spoon (1705).

Britannia and the profile of a lion's head erased (torn off at the neck). Makers were required to register new makers' marks showing the first two letters of their surnames rather than the initials of their Christian names and surnames.

SHEFFIELD PLATE

The development of Sheffield plate by Thomas Bolsover, in the early 1740s, paved the way for the growing merchant classes to purchase items resembling silver for a fraction of the cost of the

A "halo" appears around the rubbed-in shield on this entrée dish (1815) when the shield is breathed upon.

real thing. When a sheet of sterling silver was bound to an ingot of copper and then fused in a furnace, the resultant metal could be rolled or hammered into sheets and made into objects. Decoration is usually flat-chased (embossed in low relief) rather than engraved, as the latter meant cutting through to the copper. In the late 18thC a method was developed for decorating Sheffield plate with an engraved crest: a hole was cut into the object and a heavily plated or solid-silver shield soldered into place. In the early 19thC a patch of pure silver foil was burnished onto Sheffield plate objects to provide a base for crests.

BRITANNIA METAL

The remaining silver plate on this Britannia metal sugar bowl (1870) still shines when polished. However, where it has worn off it appears dull, like lead, and needs replating.

Not to be confused with Britannia standard, Britannia metal is a poor-quality, pewter-like alloy, which perishes easily. First developed in the late 18thC, it consists mainly of tin to which small quantities of antimony (a metallic-looking element) and copper have been added. In the second half of the 19thC it was often electroplated to make inexpensive tableware marked "EPBM" (electroplated Britannia metal). When worn or damaged it can rarely be replated or repaired successfully, and the cost of repairs will normally be far greater than the value of a similar object in fine condition.

ELECTROPLATE

In the 1840s the introduction of commercial electroplating heralded the demise of the Sheffield plate industry. The process, which was pioneered by the Birmingham manufacturer Elkington & Co., involves covering a metal object with a thin coating of pure silver by means of

Electroplated items such as this jug (c.1865) tend to be appreciated as affordable silver-style items rather than for their intrinsic value.

electro-deposition. A variety of base metals can be employed, although copper and nickel, or a combination of the two, have been found to be the most satisfactory ones. Harsher and whiter in appearance than objects that are manufactured from Sheffield plate, which has a soft glow, electroplated wares generally mirrored the styles that were most fashionable in sterling silver.

MIXED METALS

In the late 19thC the American firms of Tiffany & Co. and Gorham Manufacturing Co. produced a number of innovative decorative objects made of silver decorated with other metals, including copper, nickel, and brass, with the copper frequently

A mixed-metal jug by Gorham Manufacturing Co. (1900).

appearing reddish and the brass appearing soft. The technique of combining mixed metals was used to great effect, especially by American makers, for naturalistic Art Nouveau-style silver and such distinctive Japanese-influenced designs as the fine jug by Gorham shown above.

However, designs were not uniquely decorative, and the mixed-metal technique was also used on more utilitarian items such as tea services. While British designs are hallmarked, in the USA and continental Europe wares made of mixed metals are clearly marked "sterling silver and other metals". Objects of this type should be cleaned carefully, as the patina is delicate and can be stripped easily.

FORMING TECHNIQUES

Understanding how silver objects are made helps collectors to assess their value and authenticity. Among the most malleable and ductile of all materials, silver can be formed into numerous shapes in a variety of ways, and it is not unusual to find a combination of techniques applied to produce a single item. The hammer has long been the indispensable tool of silversmiths, and makers producing silver today use tools and techniques not unlike those employed when the craft first developed, although mechanization has added speed and efficiency.

RAISING

The most expensive shaping technique, and one that is very labor intensive, "raising" is used primarily for producing dishes and other

Tumbler cups, such as this example of 1731, are ideally suited to production by raising.

hollow wares (articles featuring a hollow such as bowls, drinking vessels, and dishes). The silver is raised from a flat disc that has been hammered or cast from a silver ingot, then cut to size and formed into the desired shape with a series of hammer blows. The silversmith generally works in a series of rings from the centre of the base towards the rim, forcing the metal outwards and upwards over an iron block or anvil. The silver at the rim is hammered to make it thicker and stronger.

The invention of the rolling mill in the mid-18thC revolutionized the raising process and facilitated the commercial production of sheet silver, as it enabled the sheet silver

to be made in a standard gauge. When the silver is hammered it becomes harder and tougher, although the metal must be annealed – heated and then cooled – at regular intervals to strengthen it and prevent it from becoming brittle. Hammer marks, which can generally be seen on the interior of hand-raised pieces, are removed from the surface with a special broad-headed hammer to create a smooth finish. This process is known as planishing.

WORKING WITH SHEET METAL

Used mainly in the production of beakers and tankards, and of large-scale cylindrical objects, the technique of constructing an object from a sheet of silver or Sheffield plate significantly reduced both production time and cost. By this method, which was introduced commercially in the late 18thC, an oblong sheet of silver is cut to the required size and then wrapped to form a cylinder. The seam where the two sides meet, which is visible on the wine cooler below, is soldered together, and a disc of silver is soldered into the base. Careful inspection of the inside of the piece reveals the base disc, along with hammer marks. More complex features such as feet, handles, and borders are usually cast and applied. Items made of sheet silver are generally lighter than cast wares.

A soldered seam is visible on this wine cooler (c.1800), which is made from a sheet of Sheffield plate.

CASTING

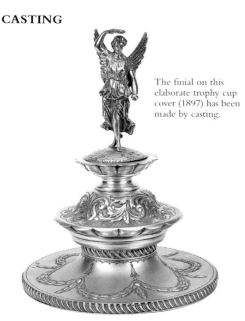

The finial on this elaborate trophy cup cover (1897) has been made by casting.

Silver objects with intricate shapes, including candlesticks, and components such as handles, finials (as above), spouts, borders, and feet, cannot be successfully raised from sheet silver and are usually cast separately. The silver is melted, poured into a mold fashioned in the desired shape, and then cooled. Once the component has solidified, it is removed from the mould, finished by hand, polished, and then soldered onto the object.

It is likely that many cast components, which often conform to a standard pattern, were supplied by specialist workshops that mass produced them for a number of silversmiths. Cast objects are usually heavier and more solid than their raised counterparts, and their undersides or insides are usually left quite rough.

WAX CASTING

The technique of wax casting, also known as *cire perdue*, involves making a wax model of the object to be produced, covering the model with clay or plaster to create a mold and then heating the mold until the wax melts. The hot wax is poured out of the mold and replaced with molten silver. Once the silver is cool, the mold is broken away.

FILIGREE

The highly decorative technique of filigree enjoyed considerable popularity throughout continental Europe during the 17thC. In Britain it was only used to a small degree in the late 17thC and again in the 19thC, when revival styles were all the rage. The technique involves twisting or plaiting fine silver wires into intricate decorative patterns of geometric or foliate ornament and then soldering these wires together. Filigree decoration is usually produced separately and applied either unsupported as an openwork border, for example on jewellery, or by being soldered onto a flat metal plate on such items as boxes or buttons.

Objects with filigree decoration are often very delicate, and the technique was usually used in the production of small items such as caddy spoons, card cases, and pill boxes. However, the technique also been used with particular success to produce large items of silver, for example candlesticks, inkstands, and caskets.

Filigree is ideally suited to the production of such small items as this caddy spoon of *c*.1800.

STAMPING

Stamping was introduced into England in the late 18thC and continues to be used for mass producing items such as bonbon dishes, photograph frames, dressing-table sets, and loaded (weighted) candlesticks. In this method, a thin sheet of silver is placed between two steel dies, with the desired pattern cut into the lower one and its opposite marked out in relief on the surface of the upper die. When mechanical pressure is applied to the top die, the silver sheet is forced between the two dies and takes on the desired shape. Items of silver that are not loaded are usually very light and flimsy and tend to be prone to damage over time.

DECORATION

The decorative style of a piece of silver provides a valuable clue to the object's date and, occasionally, its origin, particularly when the hallmarks are indistinct or absent. With the exceptions of early 18thC English silver and American silver produced throughout the 18thC, which were generally plain and unembellished, various forms of decoration were usually applied to the surface of the metal according to contemporary popular taste. New decoration was often added to an old piece of plain silver to accommodate changing trends, and engraved armorials and initials were frequently removed and replaced with new ones. The ability to identify contemporary decoration is extremely useful, because decoration added at a later date can reduce the value of a piece of silver considerably. Traditional designs have been reproduced by machine from the 19thC.

ENGRAVING

The technique of engraving involves cutting a decorative pattern by removing metal from the surface with a sharp tool called a "burin" or "graver". The style of the work frequently provides a valuable clue as to whether the engraving was done at the time of manufacture or added at a later date. Some of the finest engraving was produced in continental Europe, particularly in the 17th and early 18thC in The Netherlands and Germany where engravers were inspired by fashionable prints.

An extremely versatile technique, engraving was most commonly used for crests, armorials, initials, and inscriptions and was especially suited to such large items as the salver (1940) shown left and wine coolers with generous surface areas; on many items the engraving is featured within a decorative cartouche. In armorials the form of the shield and the design of the cartouche can provide important evidence for determining the date of a piece that has not been fully hallmarked, and occasionally it is possible to trace the arms to a particular individual, which adds to the interest and may also add to the value.

An engraved coat-of-arms was sometimes removed (polished out or erased) and replaced with a new one when silver changed hands, leaving the metal thin and weak. Coats-of-arms that have been re-engraved or added at a later date to an earlier cartouche will be more sharply defined than earlier engraving.

BRIGHT-CUT ENGRAVING

Bright-cut engraving as seen on this tea-caddy of 1796 was a popular form of decoration at the end of the 18thC, especially for Neo-classical ornament. It is identical in execution to engraving, but the design is carved at an angle with a burnished steel chisel, creating facets on the surface of the metal that reflect the light at different angles and add a sparkle to the decoration. The facets are easily worn away by polishing, and such wear is detrimental to the value – bright-cut engraving adds to the value only if it is still crisp.

CHASING

Popular at the end of the 17thC and again in the mid-18thC, chasing, as featured on the salver shown above, is the highly skilled art of hammering metal to create a form of relief. The metal is displaced (but not removed) into the decorative pattern with a chasing tool – a blunt or ball-pointed chisel or punch. The impression of the chased pattern can often be seen on the reverse or underside of the piece. Chasing is often referred to as "flat-chasing".

The most common decorative motifs included flowers, foliage, and scrolls of various types, and during the Victorian period the plain surfaces of earlier silver items were frequently lavishly chased to satisfy the prevailing taste for excessive ornament. With silver chased at the time of manufacture, hallmarks were added after the piece had been decorated, and any later decoration was generally superimposed on the hallmarks. Paul de Lamerie and Aymé Videau are among the 18thC silversmiths celebrated for the exceptional quality of their chasing.

EMBOSSING

The technique of embossing, also known as "repoussé" work, involves hammering a piece of silver from the back with decorative punches or dies to create a relief pattern. Detail and definition are added by chasing on the front of the relief design. The embossed decoration is visible on the reverse of the Victorian rosebowl (1890) shown above. European 17thC Baroque silver was often decorated with embossed flower and fruit motifs. By the 19thC embossing had fallen out of fashion, in favor of faster, more cost-effective die-stamping.

MATTING

For a matte effect to be achieved, silver is worked with small hammers to create a compact pattern of tiny dots and render a surface dull. Matting was especially popular in England and Germany in the mid-17thC. It was used to great effect on beakers to simulate sharkskin, as in the above example (*c*.1800). Matting was also used in producing background decoration to give an impression of depth.

ENAMELING

This clock (*c*.1895) by Liberty & Co. is typical of the enameled silver favored by devotees of the Arts and Crafts style. The process

of enameling involves applying a paste or oil-based mixture of metallic oxides to make a glaze. When fired, the glaze fuses onto the surface of the object, creating a colorful decorative effect. In the Victorian and Edwardian periods the technique was popular for decorating small silver objects, such as vesta, card and cigarette cases, clocks, and perfume bottles, which were often embellished with inlaid enamel plaques painted with hunting scenes, stories from Classical mythology, erotic images and landscapes. Enameling is easily chipped, which will lower the value.

PLIQUE-A-JOUR ENAMELING

Rarely found on English silver, *plique-à-jour* is a form of enameling that was particularly popular for small objects such as spoons and ladles, notably in Scandinavia, France, and Russia. The enamel is contained in an unbacked metal framework, which creates the effect of a stained-glass window. This technique was especially favored for items decorated in the delicate and sinuous Art Nouveau style, such as the case shown above (*c.*1900).

GUILLOCHE ENAMELING

In *guilloché* enameling the silver is engraved or engine-turned and then covered with a layer of translucent enamel, which allows the decorative design to shine through to shimmering effect, as on this pill box of 1934.

ENGINE-TURNING

In engine-turning, introduced at the end of the 18thC, machine-driven lathes are used to carve lines into the surface of the silver, creating a textured effect. The most common designs are waves, rosettes, and braids.

NIELLO

The niello technique seen on this spoon (Moscow, 1875) was originally used by the Romans. A black compound consisting of

silver, lead, copper, and sulphur is first heated and then reduced to a powder. A design is cut out of the silver, filled with the black compound, and heated until the powder granules fuse together. The object is polished down after firing, leaving the carved decoration filled with niello and the surface smooth. As niello is a metallic alloy, it is stronger than enamel and less prone to damage. Most examples of niello found today have been made outside Britain and the USA – many are from France, Russia, and the former Austro-Hungarian Empire – and date from the 18th to the early 20thC.

APPLIED WORK

Applied decoration describes ornament that is not part of the basic form of an object. One technique is Celtic strapwork, featured on the cream jug (1932) shown above. Another distinctive applied technique is "cut-card" work, developed in the late 17thC and perfected in the early 18thC by Huguenot craftsmen.

Cut-card work involves cutting a decorative shape from a thin sheet or card of silver, and then soldering it to the body of the vessel. Cast ornament may also be applied, as may beaded or reeded wires, soldered around the body or applied to the rim, foot, and edges for decoration and strength.

PIERCED WORK

The technique of piercing entails making tiny cuts through the silver either to create a purely decorative design, as on this basket of 1789, or for a more practical purpose such as to make holes in the top of a sugar caster. The tedious and time-consuming process, which was carried out by hand until the late 18thC, initially involved using a chisel to punch out the patterns. From the 1770s this was done with a fretsaw. Hand piercing was eventually replaced by mechanical piercing, which dramatically reduced the time and cost required to produce objects with pierced decoration.

In the 18thC pierced decoration was favored for all manner of decorative tableware, including épergnes, mustard pots, salt cellars with colorful glass liners, dish rings, and cake baskets. Hand-pierced decoration tends to be slightly rough, while machine-piercing is usually more precise and consistent. The thin-gauge silver used from the late 18thC is vulnerable to damage if pierced.

PARCEL GILDING

Silver has frequently been gilded to make it resemble gold, as well as to protect it from tarnishing. The term "parcel gilt" is used to refer to an object made of silver that has been partially covered with a gold deposit, such as this jug made in 1842. When restricted to specific areas of an object, this technique is often used to great effect for highlighting decoration and distinguishing it from the background. The dangerous early method of mercury gilding had been replaced by the safer technique of electrogilding by the mid-19thC. Silver drinking vessels were often gilded on the inside to preserve the metal from corrosion caused by the acid present in wine.

DIE STAMPING

Die-stamped silver objects such as this caddy spoon, made in 1789, are created by pressing sheet silver into a mold and forcing it into the desired shape of the mold by means of punches or drop hammers. The dies were originally made by skilled craftsmen known as "die sinkers". With the advent of machine production in the late 18thC, the process became an especially fast and efficient method of reproducing a design or object. It was also a relatively inexpensive technique, encouraging manufacturers to mass produce whole objects, such as spoons and forks, cost effectively, as well as elaborate decorative surfaces. Used extensively throughout the 19thC, die-stamping was also a favored method for manufacturing handles and feet in Sheffield plate. These components were stamped in halves, filled with lead and then applied to the object. As the metal is stretched through the die-stamping technique, it may be very thin and vulnerable to wear. Sometimes holes may be present, especially on objects featuring relief decoration.

HALLMARKS

As coins can easily be converted into silver objects and vice versa, procedures have been set up over the centuries to guarantee the purity of precious-metal alloys. Marks signifying the legal standard of pure silver, the maker, the location of assay (or testing) and the official who verified the quality of the silver were developed in most European countries. The English hallmarking system has changed little since it was introduced in 1300, when the Worshipful Company of Goldsmiths was granted permission to enforce assay laws from the Goldsmiths' Hall (hence the name "hallmark") in London. Assay offices were established across the country, although only five are in operation today, in London, Birmingham, Dublin, Edinburgh, and Sheffield. Although marking systems were established in Scotland, Ireland and continental Europe, the standards for silver varied. Assaying has always applied to both the main body and any detachable parts.

STERLING SILVER

British sterling silver usually bears at least four marks – the maker's mark, standard mark, town mark, and date letter – although there is some variation depending on the period in which an item was produced. Some items, such as the one above, also bear a commemorative mark – in this case for the 1935 Golden Jubilee of George V and Queen Mary.

An alloy of silver, copper, and other trace elements that in Britain has a purity of 92.5% silver, sterling was established as the legal standard for wrought silver in the 13thC. In 1300 Edward I introduced the requirement for the use of a hallmark to prevent fraud. Makers' marks later became mandatory. The addition of a date-letter mark, using only 20 letters of the alphabet and changing annually, identified the year the object was assayed and probably made. This standard is still enforced by the regulating guild, the Worshipful Company of Goldsmiths. Marks used to commemorate a public event or an anniversary are optional and not strictly hallmarks. In Britain marks have been used to commemorate, for example, the coronation of Elizabeth II in 1953 and her Silver Jubilee in 1977.

LEOPARD'S HEAD

From 1300 London-made sterling silver was marked with the leopard's head, which from 1478 was within a shield and wore a beard and crown. In 1544 the lion passant was adopted as the silver hallmark, and the leopard's head became the London assay office mark.

LION PASSANT

Taken from the royal arms, the mark of the lion passant supplemented the leopard's head in 1544 to designate silver of the legally required sterling standard. This mark was adopted by the Goldsmiths' Company during the reign of Henry VIII, after the coinage had been debased to contain less silver than sterling standard, and silversmiths were eager to reassure their patrons of the quality of the metal they were using. In 1720 the lion passant was taken up by the provincial English assay offices, and by those in Sheffield and Birmingham when they opened in 1773. The form of the lion changed slightly over the centuries.

BRITANNIA STANDARD

During the English Civil War, huge amounts of silver were melted down and converted to coinage to pay troops. As a result, after the Restoration of the Monarchy in 1660 the demand for domestic silver was so great that coins were melted down to fill the demand. This practice was made illegal in 1697 with the introduction of the higher Britannia standard (95.8% pure silver) preventing silversmiths from using sterling-standard silver (ie coins) and compelling them to use a metal with a higher silver content, preventing coin clipping or melting. Wares made from Britannia standard silver are identified by a mark with the figure of Britannia and the lion's head erased (torn off at the neck).

OTHER MARKS
PROVINCIAL MARKS

Outside London, a number of smaller towns marked their own silver. Since provincial marking was relatively haphazard and inconsistent compared with that in London, pieces featuring relatively rare or unusual provincial marks are usually highly prized among collectors.

Birmingham was a very important center for silver production during the late 18thC, especially for such small items as buckles and vinaigrettes. An assay office was opened there in 1773, with the town mark designated by an anchor.

In the 17thC marking was introduced into Ireland. As the marking system there tended to be arbitrary, Irish silver does not always bear complete marks. The crowned harp was Dublin's town mark from 1637, and in 1731 the figure of Hibernia was added.

Marks on Scottish silver were introduced in the mid-15thC. The town mark of Edinburgh, instituted in 1485, is a castle with three towers. In 1759 a thistle replaced the assay master's mark in Edinburgh.

DUTY MARKS

To help offset the staggering costs of the American War of Independence (1775–83), increased duty was imposed on British silver. A new mark, featuring the monarch's head in profile within an escutcheon, was introduced in 1784 as proof that duty had been paid to the government at the time of assay. The heads of successive reigning sovereigns appeared on English silver until the duty was abolished in 1890.

IMPORT MARKS

The Customs Act of 1842 made it illegal to import gold or silver wares into Great Britain and Ireland unless they had been assayed at a British office. From 1867 silver articles produced outside Britain were assigned a distinctive mark of foreign origin – the letter "F" within an oval escutcheon – in addition to the standard British hallmarks. After 1904 imported silver was stamped with a symbol designating the decimal value of the standard used.

CONTINENTAL EUROPEAN SILVER MARKS

Silver produced in continental Europe was not marked as systematically as English silver, although marks were employed to signify quality or during periods when duty was payable. However, town marks were frequently used, and these may furnish valuable clues for determining the date and place of manufacture of an item of silver. With silver produced in France, for example, each component of a piece – such as the main body and any detachable parts such as handles, lids and finials – should feature a separate set of marks.

AMERICAN MARKS

There is no official marking system in the USA, and the only assay office was one operating in Baltimore from 1814 until 1830. However, most makers stamped their silver with abbreviated or full maker or company names, as on the example above, which also features the scratched pattern number, the standard of silver used and a "C" for Charles T. Cook (company president 1902–7).

Emblems, such as the double-headed lion reminiscent of a lion passant on this mark by Whiting Manufacturing Co., were used by many makers. The shape of the enclosure around the mark can help establish where or when an item was made, as shapes varied with place of production and period. Some firms also used their own date marks or stamped wares with their weight in ounces.

COPIES, FAKES & ALTERATIONS

As a result of their intrinsic value, objects of silver and gold have been copied and faked for centuries. The popular enthusiasm for historical silver became more widespread from the 19thC, leading to the faking of large and valuable objects. Ewers, coffeepots, and punchbowls, as well as smaller pieces such as apostle spoons and mugs, have long been copied to meet the demand for good-quality silver, especially in the face of dwindling supplies of such. Designs and patterns regularly changed according to the dictates of fashion and taste, and silversmiths answered the desire for new styles by adapting old-fashioned silver. Faithful copies and reproductions of earlier silverware designs are recognized and accepted as legitimate, as no effort is made to deceive, and these objects can be identified by their hallmarks. The fraudulent practice of passing off as original a cast reproduction of a silver object that appears to include the original hallmark is a most common form of faking.

COPIES

Sometimes silver objects are cast from originals, with the old hallmark deleted and new marks applied. This practice of copying is perfectly acceptable. However, reproducing an item complete only with its original hallmarks – a practice that is possible due to effective modern casting techniques – demonstrates an intent to deceive and is highly illegal.

FAKES

Pieces intended to deceive (for example, a reproduction of a Fabergé egg complete with "original" marks) are generally easy to detect. The craftsmanship and quality of detail of a master cannot be reproduced by mass-production methods, and the lack of quality is often self-evident in a piece of faked silver.

Forged marks, produced with brass punches rather than the standard hard steel punches of the assay offices, can be identified by soft outlines and lack of definition. The most common method of faking silver involves removing the marks from an older or a more valuable item, or one by a celebrated maker that is in poor condition, and then soldering them into a less-valuable piece. Most types of object have characteristic configurations of hallmarks. For example, mustard pots are usually marked in a group on the base, while salvers are nearly always marked in a straight line. Marks that have been added or "let in" are often positioned incorrectly, distorted or missing altogether. The uncharacteristic slanted line of the George III hallmarks on the Victorian rosebowl featured above, for example, suggests that they are a spurious addition.

DUTY DODGERS

In the 18thC, and especially after 1720 when duty on silver was significantly increased, the practice known as "duty dodging" was widespread in Britain. It involved transposing

hallmarks from damaged or redundant pieces of silver, particularly from the late 17thC, into newly made items of silver to avoid paying the high duty, or tax, that had been levied on wrought plate.

High-quality small pieces of silver were sent to the assay office for marking; dodgers then removed the marks and inserted them into unassayed larger objects, which could mean considerable savings as the duty payable was determined partly by weight. On the unassayed teapot (shown left) the silversmith has let-in, or inserted, a hallmarked silver disc cut from a piece of redundant 18thC silver into the base (shown in detail), thereby avoiding paying duty on the teapot's total weight.

ALTERATIONS

The enduring quality of sterling silver made it a natural target for alterations and modifications according to prevailing fashions.

Any alteration to an original piece of silver, whether in function or decoration, will significantly reduce the value.

These alterations become illegal if the original purpose of the item has been changed, for example if a mug has been made into a jug. Recognizing reconstructed silver items should prove easier the more familiar the collector becomes with the forms and decorative styles of various periods.

The practice of altering silver reached its peak during the Victorian period, when the popular taste was for lavishly decorated and ornate objects. At this time many 17th and 18thC plain silver vessels were chased beyond recognition with lavish ornament of flowers and foliage.

It has also been common practice across the centuries to alter or convert silver items from redundant pieces into useful ones. Many tankards, for example, were converted into teapots when tea became more popularly drunk than beer in the 18thC.

Silver goblets are also prime candidates for alterations because of their plain form, which is easy to embellish or adapt. In the example left, a hot-water jug has been fashioned from a Neo-classical silver goblet (1788) by the addition of an insulated handle, an upper body, cover, and lip decorated with a gadrooned rim. The awkward proportions and placement of the marks provide valuable clues as to how this piece has been reconstructed. Hot-water jugs are usually marked on the base or near to the rim, and on this example the marks suspiciously appear beneath the rim – where they would normally be found on a goblet.

Cream jugs are among the easiest silver vessels to alter. Many small christening mugs such as the above example (1840) have been converted by the addition of a spout, but these are usually easy to recognize by their unbalanced proportions and rough patches around joins. This type of alteration is illegal unless the spout has been hallmarked, and there is no intention to deceive a buyer.

Other signs of alteration include crude joins suggested by roughly soldered patches (typical on hollow wares) and thin, vulnerable patches of metal, where an original inscription may have been polished off to make way for new engraving. Pushing gently on a suspicious patch will reveal if any original engraving has been removed. All detachable components of a piece should be at least partly marked. Check all detachable parts such as handles, feet, and finials very carefully.

PART 4

SILVER FILE

ABOVE A NEO-CLASSICAL-STYLE CANDLESTICK,
c.1900, $4,000–4,800.

LEFT AN ART DECO PARCEL-GILDED COCKTAIL SET,
c.1930, $3,200–6,400.

Candlesticks are among the most common collectible items of silver, which is of little surprise since they were used daily as a source of illumination. However, candlesticks made before the mid-17thC are rare, as most were melted down for coin or because they were worn. The earliest surviving candlesticks were raised from thin sheet metal and are usually very light. By the late 17thC the sophisticated but expensive technique of casting candlesticks in solid silver had been developed by skilled Huguenot craftsmen, who fled from France after the Revocation of the Edict of Nantes in 1685. By the 1770s mechanization was facilitating the more economical production of "loaded" candlesticks stamped from rolled sheet silver, with the bases weighted for stability with pitch, wood, or plaster of Paris; vast numbers of loaded candlesticks were produced in Sheffield and Birmingham, thus becoming accessible to a wider clientele – early candlesticks were used primarily by the upper classes and the Church. Similar to candlesticks, but smaller and more portable, are chambersticks, used at night to light the way to the bedchamber. Implements used in conjunction with candlesticks, to snuff out candles, trim wicks, or melt wax, are diverse. However, the functional (as opposed to decorative) role of candlesticks and their accessories means that many are in poor condition. Candelabra, which mirror the same styles as candlesticks, are generally more valuable and better preserved. The earliest ones are from the mid-17thC, although most now available are from the late 18th and 19thC.

EARLY CANDLESTICKS

Early (pre-1750) English candlesticks are rare, since many were melted down for coin during the Civil War (1642–9) or restored to circulation in another form if worn. Made of light sheet silver, most early candlesticks were designed with large bases to counterbalance their instability; decoration was typically minimal. From the 1680s casting sparked the production of heavier, taller, more ornate designs that could stand on small bases. Most candlesticks were made in pairs and are still sold as such today. Few American examples were made prior to 1760.

▲ 17THC DESIGNS
One of a pair, this Charles II candlestick by Benjamin Prosser (1670) is an example of mid-17thC transitional design. Candlesticks at this period were made from thin sheet metal and are consequently very light; the short baluster stem on a proportionally large, broad base was designed to prevent the candle from toppling over. Here, the square base has been raised, but the stem has been cast. Early candlesticks such as this are usually very plain, with decoration limited to an engraved armorial or embossed trailing flowers. $32,000–40,000 (for a pair)

◀ HUGUENOT INFLUENCE

The introduction of casting methods from the 1680s influenced candlestick design. Casting facilitated the production of more sophisticated decoration, as on this pair of William and Mary candlesticks made in 1694. However, casting was a costly technique, as the base was cast separately from the column – the latter being cast in two halves – and the separate parts then had to be soldered together. $13,120–19,200

EDICT OF NANTES

Issued by Henry IV in 1598, the Edict of Nantes gave freedom of religion to French Protestants (Huguenots). In 1685 it was revoked by Louis XI; this caused many Huguenots to flee to Britain and The Netherlands to avoid persecution. The skills Huguenot silversmiths brought with them proved an important influence on the silver trade in Britain.

▶ DORIC FLUTED COLUMNS

These Queen Anne candlesticks in the shape of Doric fluted columns (1703) are late survivors of a style that was fashionable in England before the cast baluster form was introduced by the Huguenots in the 1680s. Made from sheet silver and hollow throughout, they are lighter and more vulnerable to damage than cast examples and much less expensive to make. The drip-pan at the base of the stem – designed to protect the hand from burning wax – gradually became smaller and was absorbed as a decorative feature. $8,000–12,800

QUEEN ANNE STYLE

- **Reign period** (1702–14)
- **Dates** prevalent style in England from *c.*1688 until *c.*1720 (and, with increased ornament, until *c.*1730)
- **Metal** many wares were made in Britannia standard silver (finer and softer than sterling silver) – the enforced higher standard (95.8% pure silver) between 1697 and 1720
- **Technique** mostly casting, inspired by Huguenot silversmiths
- **Forms** typically plain with clean lines; bases: generally small, canted oblong, or octagonal; stems: usually baluster
- **Decoration** minimal, at most perhaps a coat-of-arms or an armorial; little applied ornament; faceting popular to reflect light
- **Revival** late 19th/early 20thC

LATER CANDLESTICKS I

In the early 18thC plain candlesticks came into fashion again. By the 1730s they had become increasingly tall, and from the 1740s many had detachable nozzles that could be cleaned easily. By the mid-18thC lavishly decorated "Rococo" candlesticks were made, and by the late 18thC examples of loaded sheet silver, Sheffield plate, or cast silver were being produced in huge numbers, either in the plain baluster style on a circular foot, or in the form of a Corinthian column on a square plinth. The growth of industrial centres such as Birmingham and Sheffield and mechanization allowed silversmiths to mass produce candlesticks inexpensively to suit the demands of the newly affluent middle classes. After the opening of the assay offices in Sheffield and Birmingham in 1773, production of loaded candlesticks mushroomed.

◀ **EARLY 18THC DESIGNS**
Candlesticks made at the beginning of the 18thC tend to be plain with minimal decoration, a canted square or octagonal base and a baluster square column. The engraved coat-of-arms on the base of this early George II candlestick, produced in 1727 by Anthony Nelme, is the only embellishment. The edges of the base and column are slightly rounded, which indicates that this example has probably been used extensively. $6,400–9,600

PARTS OF A CANDLESTICK

Candlesticks were made in a diverse range of sizes and styles, but the basic form of a base, vertical stem, nozzle and, on most examples, a drip pan of some description is essentially the same. Many candlesticks made in the Queen Anne style, such as this George I candlestick by the London maker Matthew Cooper (1718), were made in Britannia standard silver – a higher standard than sterling and the legal standard from 1697 until 1720. $8,000– 16,000 (for a pair)

The detachable nozzle fits into the socket to hold the candle and stop the wax dripping down the inside of the stem. Detachable nozzles, which could be cleaned, were typical from the 1740s. The shape of the nozzle usually mirrors that of the base.

The candlestick stem is also known as the column. This example has an engraved armorial at the stem base.

Some candlesticks feature a ledge above the nozzle that catches dripping wax and is known as a drip-pan; others feature a tray between the stem and the base to catch drips.

The socket (often known as the sconce or capital) is the cylindrical holder, attached to the top of the column, that the candle fits into.

A protruding ornament on the stem is called the knop.

The lowest part of the candlestick is known as the base.

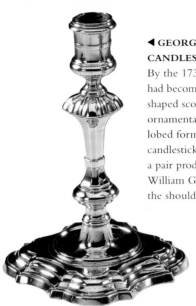

◀ GEORGE II CANDLESTICKS

By the 1730s candlesticks had become taller, with spool-shaped sconces and richer ornamentation of pleated or lobed forms. This George II candlestick, which is one of a pair produced in 1740 by William Gould, has fluting on the shoulders and turned work around the center of the base, but is still rather restrained and symmetrical compared to later Rococo examples. Some silversmiths specialized in the production of candlesticks in the mid-18thC, the Cafe and Gould families, both of whom were based in London, being among the best known. $2,400–4,000 (for a pair)

▶ ROCOCO STYLE

The influence of the exuberant French Rococo can be seen on these George II candlesticks, which are part of an extremely valuable set of four made in 1750 by the London-based Huguenot silversmith Paul Crespin (1694–1770). Cast and chased with opulent ornament, these candlesticks testify to the highly extravagant designs that adorned the tables of the wealthy at this time. Other leading contemporary British silversmiths include Paul de Lamerie and James Shruder. $64,000–96,000 (for a set of four)

◀ LATE 18THC CANDLESTICKS

Towards the end of the 18thC the introduction of Neo-classicism brought about changes in candlestick design, including the use of square bases, Corinthian column stems with urn-shaped nozzles and restrained Classical ornament such as gadrooning, swags, beading, reeding, and stylized foliage. Influential architects such as Robert Adam produced candlestick designs in the Neo-classical style as part of complete schemes for interior decoration. The growth of industrialization in centres including Sheffield and Birmingham enabled silversmiths to mass produce such candlesticks as this loaded pair (part of a set of four made in 1777 by Makepeace & Carter) inexpensively to accommodate the demands of the newly affluent middle classes. $4,800–6,400 (for a set of four)

LATER CANDLESTICKS II

In the Regency period (*c*.1790–1820) candlesticks became increasingly ornate, with lavish scrolls and foliage applied to the base, around the socket and at the top of the stem. From *c*.1820 many 17th and 18thC styles were revived, with the Rococo taste especially popular. Reflecting the Victorian penchant for novelty decoration, figural candlesticks in the form of rustic figures of shepherds, caryatids, or knights in armour were also fashionable during the 19thC, and in the late 19thC there was a revival of column candlesticks, decorated with diverse border patterns. In reaction against mass-production and very heavy reliance on historical styles, and inspired by the asymmetry of the newly accessible Japanese art, in the late 19thC a number of British and American silversmiths produced handmade wares with the emphasis on fine craftsmanship, quality materials and simple, honest design. Known as the Arts and Crafts Movement, this coincided in continental Europe with the avant-garde Art Nouveau Movement, which was inspired by the flowing lines of nature and asymmetrical design.

REVIVAL STYLES

A multitude of historical styles were popularly revived in the Victorian period (1837–1901), including Gothic, Rococo, and Neo-classical. Eclecticism – where motifs from different periods were combined – was also in vogue.

▶ **REGENCY DESIGNS**
This silver-gilt baluster Regency candlestick on a circular foot has been cast and applied with Classical ornament of bands of stylized acanthus foliage. The value of this candlestick, which is one of a set of four made by John Scofield in 1791, is considerably enhanced by its excellent quality. $96,000–128,000 (for a set of four)

◀ **ROCOCO REVIVAL**
This pair of Sheffield plate candlesticks (1819) by John Watson is opulently decorated with scrolls, shells, and stems in the form of entwined dolphins – typical of the Rococo style. However, the excessive ornament seen here is in the high Rococo taste and lacks the lightness and balance of the 18thC originals. Unlike the earlier cast examples (*see* p.55), most revival candlesticks were made of loaded sheet silver. $2,400–4,000 (for a pair)

◀ CAST ROCOCO-STYLE DESIGNS

Compared with the Sheffield-made loaded candlestick shown below left, this George III example, which is one of a pair made in 1819 by John Cradock and William K. Reid of London, is of exceptionally fine quality. Cast and heavily chased in the Rococo manner, the baluster stems and urn-shaped capitals have been decorated with an abundance of swirling shells, scrolls, rockwork, flowers, foliage, and dog-mask ornament. By the end of the 19thC very few candlesticks were cast, largely because the technique had become prohibitively expensive, and the new mechanized methods for manufacturing were much more practical. $16,000–24,000 (for a pair)

▶ ART NOUVEAU

The distinctive silver designs by Archibald Knox for the London firm of Liberty & Co. in the late 19th and early 20thC are well loved by collectors. This example draws upon a floral design in its witty evocation of a flowering plant – such naturalistic motifs and sinewy lines are typical of the Art Nouveau style. $4,800–6,400 (for a pair)

◀ ARTS AND CRAFTS

This candlestick is one of a pair made in 1905 by the firm of James Dixon & Sons. The clean, geometric lines are characteristic of the Arts and Crafts Movement, which was championed in Britain by William Morris and harked back to quality craftsmanship and simple design in the face of industrial mass-production. The minimal decoration of rivets is typical. $1,920–2,400 (for a pair)

MARKS

This is one of several marks used by the Sheffield firm of James Dixon & Sons (est. 1806; known from 1835 as James Dixon & Sons). Wares also feature numerals representing pattern numbers and in some cases a trumpet trademark.

J • D & S

LATER CANDLESTICKS III

Twentieth-century candlesticks encompass a host of styles, from the tail-end of Arts and Crafts and Art Nouveau through to Art Deco, historical revivals, and minimalist modern design. Most contemporary candlesticks were made in pairs or sets of four, which makes it difficult for collectors to build up larger sets. Some candlesticks have matching accessories such as snuffers, and a complete set will be worth more than a single piece. Styles of candlestick from the 1950s and later are generally not popular and have a limited appeal, meaning that some can be found at reasonable prices. An important factor with candlesticks is that any detachable parts match the main body in style, date, and maker's mark.

◀ CLEAN LINES

This 20thC candlestick is one of a pair by the Danish silversmith Georg Jensen (1866–1935), whose designs are still made by the Jensen factory. As if turned on a lathe, the round knurled base is echoed by a circular drip tray below the candle socket. $4,800–5,600 (for a pair)

◀ REVIVAL STYLES

Adaptations of historical styles were a feature of Art Deco metalwork. This candlestick from the 1930s is a rather simplified version of a Neo-classical form popular in the late18thC, but it lacks the elegance and fine detail of its earlier counterparts. $480–640 (for a pair)

▶ STUART DEVLIN

This candlestick and snuffer are from a set of four candlesticks and a snuffer by Stuart Devlin. Australian-born Devlin has been based in London since 1965, and in 1982 was made Goldsmith and Jeweller to Queen Elizabeth II. These candlesticks, which are typical of 1970s design, feature textured stems that directly reverse the form of the snuffer. $480–640 (for a set of four with snuffer)

▶ MASS-PRODUCTION

The tapering baluster-shaped stem is typical of most late 19th and 20thC candlesticks, but this version is quite plain, with bands of die-stamped floral decoration around the domed base, shoulder and socket. Such contemporary candlesticks were manufactured in large quantities and are readily available to collectors. $400–480 (for a pair)

TAPERSTICKS

Tapersticks, which were made from the late 17thC, were designed to hold a taper or thin candle and used to melt sealing wax at a writing desk, light a tobacco pipe, or provide illumination. Most were in the form of small candlesticks, measuring approximately only 4in (10cm) in height; early examples are usually cast and mirror the style of contemporary candlesticks. However, some tapersticks were made in the form of chambersticks, often also with a candle extinguisher. Tapersticks were generally made in pairs but rarely survive as such, particularly early 18thC examples. In the mid-18thC they were replaced by waxjacks.

◀ **POPULAR DESIGNS**
Made by John Crouch of London (1766), this George III taperstick on a shaped square base is in a popular form that was made in many variations. Some tapersticks incorporated inkstands; others were made to match candlesticks. $640–960

◀ **SURVIVING PAIRS**
Tapersticks are rarer than candlesticks and very sought after. A surviving pair, such as this one by John Cafe of London (1745), is particularly desirable. As tapersticks are small and fragile, they are prone to damage, which will considerably diminish their value. They are almost always marked under the base. $2,400–4,000

▶ **VICTORIAN DESIGNS**
Small ornamental chamber-style tapersticks such as this one (1842) were popular for the desk or writing table.

This example has a conical extinguisher commonly found on chambersticks and is decorated with stamped foliage and scrolls. $400–560

◀ **EXTINGUISHERS AND SNUFFERS**
This late Victorian taperstick by William Comyns (1897) is in the form of a chamberstick with an extinguisher. Original conical extinguishers or snuffers add to the value; replacement ones are quite common and will detract from the value. $320–400

SNUFFERS, WAXJACKS & CHAMBERSTICKS

Scissor-shaped snuffers were essential for trimming and collecting the wicks of tallow candles, which burnt more quickly than wax candles and needed to be frequently trimmed. Many had steel blades and a box-like device at the end to hold pieces of wick. They were produced, by specialist makers, together with a small oblong tray or a stand that was sometimes made en suite with a candlestick. Sometimes snuffer trays are now sold as pen trays. Waxjacks were devices designed to hold a coiled wax taper, so that the end of the taper pointed upwards and the flame could be used to melt sealing wax. Chambersticks lit the way to the bedchamber at night and were made small for safety. They were produced in large sets, because they were required by each member of the household. The central socket for the candle is mounted in a circular dish designed to catch the hot dripping wax, and this is usually decorated with reeding, shells, beading, or gadrooned ornament. Early chambersticks have long, flat handles, but few survive. More common are later ones with ring or scroll handles, which were introduced in the 1720s; some designs had a socket for a conical extinguisher or a pierced slot to hold scissor-action snuffers.

◀ SNUFFER STANDS

Early 18thC snuffer stands usually mirror the style of contemporary candlesticks, with a faceted baluster stem and base and an engraved armorial as the only decoration. The scissor-like snuffers were contained upright inside the body. Some snuffer stands feature a hook at the front of the body to support a candle extinguisher. As the design of this early George II example, which was made by Matthew Cooper in 1729, is more commonly found on snuffers from the late Queen Anne period (c.1710–14), this snuffer stand may have been produced to match a pair of earlier candlesticks or to replace an original stand. Watch out for splitting around joins at the handle or the base of the stem, and for solder repairs, as any such damage will reduce the value of the piece. $8,000–12,800

▶ SNUFFER TRAYS

In the mid-18thC snuffers had "waisted" or oblong-shaped stands, like trays, such as this fine example with matching snuffers by James Shruder (1745). Later trays, in oval or boat shapes, were made from flat sheet silver, often with applied pierced borders. Although more common, these tend to be more lightly made than early examples. A tray and matching pair of scissor-action snuffers are rarely found together and fetch a premium. $8,000–12,800

◀ SCISSOR-ACTION SNUFFERS

Snuffers such as these mid-19thC plated ones could be picked up easily and used to snuff out a flame and were made in large quantities in the 19thC. Some snuffers cut and collected the end of the wick in a box, although this was no longer necessary with the invention of the self-consuming wick c.1800. $48–64

▶ WAXJACKS

Waxjacks held a coil of wax, so that the taper pointed upwards and gave a small flame for melting sealing wax when lit. This elegant circular example (1778) on lion-paw feet is constructed with a central rod around which the taper coils vertically with the end in a pincer-like grip. It is imaginatively embellished with decoration of beaded rims and a wavy-fluted finial, and the cone-shaped snuffer is suspended from a silver chain. Waxjacks replaced tapersticks from the mid-18thC. $2,400–4,000

▲ CHAMBERSTICKS

Chambersticks were made in large numbers in both silver and Sheffield plate from the 1770s. Those in Sheffield plate were less expensive than those made in London and as a result tend to be light and of poorer quality. The simple gadrooned border featured on this example from 1810 was a very common decorative motif from the mid-18th to the early 19thC; decoration is usually stamped and applied rather than cast. $640–960

CHAMBERSTICK HALLMARKS

All the detachable parts of the chamberstick, such as the nozzle, extinguisher, and base of the tray, should bear the same marks as the main body.

CANDELABRA

Candelabra – table candlesticks with branches for holding extra lights – were first made in the mid-17thC, although most surviving examples date from the late 18thC and 19thC. They mirror the styles of contemporary candlesticks, and were commonly made in pairs. Early candelabra had two branches, but those made at the end of the 18thC, when the main meal was taken after dark and more light was required, had three branches. Some massive, extremely elaborate silver-gilt candelabra were produced during the Regency period (c.1790–1820), usually as part of lavish table centerpieces. In the 19thC it became fashionable to make candelabra with five or more branches. As they were of better quality and more valuable than candlesticks, candelabra did not generally suffer the same harsh wear or damage, and on the whole many candelabra on the market today are found in relatively good condition.

▶ **SHEFFIELD PLATE**

This George III candelabrum, which was made in Sheffield by John Green & Co. in 1795, is characteristic of the light, elegant two-branched examples made in the late 18thC. It was common for candelabra to be produced in Sheffield plate as part of a matching set with more valuable silver candlesticks. Each detachable part – the nozzle, stem, and branches – should be in the same style and decoration and bear an identical maker's mark. $4,000–5,600 (for a pair)

▼ **ROCOCO REVIVAL**

Some of the most exceptional Rococo candelabra were made in France in the first half of the 18thC. Many 19thC silversmiths looked to the past for inspiration, and the fondness for excessive decoration at this time found its greatest expression in Rococo ornament. This William IV example is one of a very valuable pair made in 1836 by the top London firm of R. & S. Garrard. $32,000–40,000 (for a pair)

◀ **FIVE-LIGHT CANDELABRUM**

Five-light candelabra were produced from the beginning of the 19thC. The tapering reeded column of this finely made Sheffield plate example (c.1835) stands on a shaped circular base decorated in typical style with flowers and scrolls. Sometimes candelabra were altered according to changing fashions, and many were converted to oil lamps (and later, electrical lamps) when oil and electrical lighting were introduced. $960–1,280

▶ **TIFFANY & CO.**

This extraordinary showpiece (one of a unique pair made in 1884 at a cost of $780) demonstrates the superb quality attained in the late 19thC by Tiffany & Co. It has been cast and lavishly chased with mermaids astride dolphins – the stem of the pair to this example features mermen leading seahorses – and as a figural candelabrum by a major maker is extremely desirable. On candelabra with many branches, check that all the nozzles are present; missing ones are detrimental to the value. $128,000–192,000 (for a pair)

TIFFANY & CO.
Tiffany marks changed over the years. From 1873 until 1965 they included the letter or the surname of the company president, which helps collectors to date items. The "T" at the end of this mark refers to Charles L. Tiffany, president from 1891 until 1902.

▶ **ARTS AND CRAFTS**

Charles Robert Ashbee (1863–1942) was among those late 19thC Arts and Crafts designers who championed the revival of traditions of handworked metal. In 1888 he formed the Guild of Handicraft in London's East End – a working medieval-style guild where masters taught apprentices. Hammered surfaces, cabochons, enameling, and organic- and Celtic-style ornament are all characteristic of the style. This fine Arts and Crafts candelabrum was made c.1895. $12,800–16,000 (for a pair)

◀ **ART NOUVEAU**

The curving stem and sinuous candle sockets of this American silver-gilt candelabrum by Theodore Starr (c.1900) illustrate the influence of the Art Nouveau style that was introduced in the late 19thC. Its simplicity is in striking contrast to the opulent, highly decorated examples that were the cornerstone of Victorian taste. $1,600–4,800

Dining Silver

The silver for the dining-table featured in this section covers a vast range, from the most basic of dining items such as plates and flatware to elaborate dishes for serving food at the table. It includes magnificent centerpieces designed principally as vehicles for show and sometimes made as presentation gifts, multi-purpose baskets and bowls, cruet and condiment sets, and an unclassifiable collection of miscellaneous items from meat skewers to menu-card holders. In the late 17thC complete dinner services, which included matching plates, cutlery, and serving dishes, were introduced to Britain from France. By the mid-18thC the custom of dining on a grand scale demanded large and luxurious dinner services, most of which consisted of six dozen meat plates, two dozen soup plates, and a variety of attendant serving dishes made en suite. In the early 19thC many complete services were commissioned by wealthy families from such leading makers as Paul Storr, Benjamin Smith, and Philip Rundell. From the mid-19thC increased mechanization meant that silver items could be mass produced far more cost-effectively than before, with the result that a great amount of dining silver was produced at this time. It was common practice in the 19thC to alter plates by removing old borders, which were either worn or out of fashion, and applying new and usually more elaborate ones. Re-bordered plates, though technically not illegal if the new borders have been hallmarked, are best avoided, as any alteration or later decoration reduces the value.

PLATES & SOUP PLATES

With the exception of border decoration, plate design changed little in the 18th and 19thC. Early plates have broad, flat borders, are decorated with an engraved crest or coat-of-arms and are usually marked underneath. New borders were often added and rims reshaped according to contemporary fashions, and this remodeling often resulted in lost or damaged marks. By the 1840s porcelain services were popular, and most silver plates were made as additions to or replacements for earlier services.

▲ **EARLY DESIGNS**
Most early dinner plates are very plain. Hallmarks on Charles II plates such as this example of 1679 are rare; if featured they are usually on the top of the border, as seen here. Although plates are most desirable in sets (usually of 12), this example (one of a pair) is exceptional. $4,000–5,440 (for a pair)

SCRATCHWEIGHTS
Often, the number and weight of each item in a set was inscribed on its base. This may show how many items were in the set and, by a change in weight, if a piece has been altered.

N⁰ 3

69 „ 19

► DATING

Plates were rarely made in different sizes or shapes, so border decoration is generally the key to determining the date. The border on these soup plates (part of a dining service) was fashionable in the Neo-classical period. If present, scratchweights may help to determine if the plate has been remodelled. $800–960

◄ SOUP PLATES

Soup plates are distinguished from dinner plates by a deeper central well. Made by the London silversmith Philip Rollos in the Britannia standard period (1697–1720), this high- quality set of Queen Anne soup plates (1706) was originally part of a larger service made for an aristocrat. Although this rare set is desirable, in general soup plates are less valuable than dinner plates. $12,800–16,000

◄ EXTRAVAGANCE

The elaborate border on this top-quality plate by Philip Rundell (1825) was popular during the Regency (c.1790–1820). At this time, many fine silver dinner services were commissioned by aristocratic families from such leading makers as Rundell, Paul Storr and Benjamin Smith. $640–800

► MODERN PLATES

These modern plates (1932), which are similar in style to the Charles II example shown on the previous page, demonstrate how little plate design has changed over the centuries. Plates such as these, which were also produced in electroplate, are commonplace, and it is fairly easy to obtain a complete set today. $4,000– 4,800 (for a set of 12)

SERVING DISHES

Serving dishes, which were generally made en suite with plates and often formed part of a larger dinner service, were used for presenting the main course to the table. Made in a variety of designs and sizes for different purposes, the most popular versions tend to be either very large or quite small. Elongated oval platters were made to hold fish, with especially long dishes for salmon. Dishes for serving a haunch of venison are usually fairly large (17¾–23½in/ 45–60cm); they feature wells to collect all the juices from the meat and sometimes also had matching dome-shaped covers with loop handles. From the mid-18thC serving dishes were sometimes fitted with pierced inserts, known as mazarines, which were used to drain the juices from the meat or fish. Other serving wares include two-handled trays, used for serving drinks and often made with matching tea or coffee services.

◀ MEAT DISHES
This meat dish (1817), part of a set of serving dishes of varying sizes, is fairly small and was probably made to serve poultry. Although this size (12in/30cm) is common, meat dishes were produced in all sizes from 9in (22.5cm). This popular style was also made in old Sheffield plate and electroplate. Meat dishes are sometimes called platters or "meat flats". $960–1,600

▶ FISH PLATTERS
Long platters for fish, such as this late 19thC Viennese example with a reeded border, were more popular in continental Europe than in Britain. They can be fairly easily found and are affordable today. $800–1,280

◀ VENISON DISHES
This Sheffield plate serving dish (c.1840), big enough for a haunch of venison, bears the "tree and well" design that allowed meat juices to run down the channels and collect in the well. Nestled in the border is a coronet with five balls, indicating that this dish once belonged to an earl. $1,600–2,400

▶ MAZARINES

Mazarines enjoyed their greatest popularity in the mid-18thC. They are rare today, especially if still with their original serving dishes. They are very sought after, primarily for the delicate pierced decoration in a variety of patterns, including scrolls, stars, flowers, crosslets, and geometric designs. Sometimes they have pad or ball feet underneath for extra support. $1,200–1,600

◀ TWO-HANDLED TRAYS

The navette shape of this late 18thC Dutch serving tray was popular towards the end of the Neo-classical period. It was universally copied in the early 19thC, and particularly popular in England. Although heavy, two-handled trays were made in two pieces (the flat central section and the border) and are therefore flimsy. Avoid examples that are not made of solid silver. $4,800–8,000

COLLECTING

● Watch out for serving dishes that are in poor condition. Stacking may have caused denting, and an absence of scratches or knife marks may be the result of overpolishing, which will have left the silver very thin.
● Meat-dish covers are often in poor condition as a result of frequent use. They are cumbersome and require considerable storage space, which means that in general they are not very practical.

▼ MEAT-DISH COVERS

Meat-dish covers such as this electroplated example of c.1865 were placed over poultry or joints of meat to keep them hot at the table and were most popular in the early 19thC. The majority were made in old Sheffield plate or electroplate, as it was expensive to make such a large item from solid silver. They are usually oval shaped and often have decorative borders, sometimes to match serving dishes. Graduated sets fetch a premium. $160–240

ENTREE & VEGETABLE DISHES

New dining fashions introduced in France in the late 17thC, whereby diners served themselves at the table, necessitated the creation of decorative dishes from which food could be served. Made in pairs or sets, silver entrée dishes were used to keep food on a sideboard or to serve the first course of cooked food before the main meat course. They are usually shallow, with flat bottoms or four feet and handled domed covers, which were sometimes detachable, so that they could be used as separate dishes. In the mid-19thC dining customs changed again, and as it became fashionable to serve food from a sideboard rather than the table, fewer entrée dishes were made. A variation on the entrée dish, vegetable dishes are usually of shallow, circular form with high domed covers. Some have glass liners and some have dividers, which enabled several types of food to be served from the dish at once. Entrée dishes are usually used today to hold vegetables; the lids often have twist-off handles and can be used as extra dishes.

◀ **ENTREE DISHES**
Before 1800 entrée dishes were usually of oval, circular, or navette form with simple gadrooned border decoration; in the 19thC an oblong or cushion shape was favoured. Many later examples have elaborate handles, perhaps cast as crests, vegetables, or fruits. Entrée dishes such as this example of 1778 by the London maker John Kenteser should have their own well-fitting covers; bases, and covers were often scratched with a number or mark to indicate which base matched which cover. $16,000–24,000 (for a set of four)

▶ **HEATING SYSTEMS**
From the early 19thC the bases of entrée dishes were often made of silver plate and filled with boiling water or a bar of heated iron to keep the food warm. Sometimes the bases have insulated wooden feet to protect the table or sideboard from the heat. This valuable dish of 1824 by John Bridge is set in a hot-water stand by Paul Storr; it is large and heavy, with the high domed cover that was in vogue at that time. $48,00–64,000 (for a set of four)

◀ **VICTORIAN DISHES**
In the 1870s and 1880s Neo-classical-style oval entrée dishes with beaded (as on this example of 1875), scroll or reed-and-ribbon borders were popular. Heavy weight usually indicates a better piece, although watch out for old Sheffield plate dishes with lead-filled bases. Also avoid damaged or worn examples. $130–160 (for a single); $400–480 (for a pair)

S. KIRK & SON

This leading silver company in Baltimore, Maryland, was founded in 1815 by Samuel Kirk and his partner John Smith, who remained with the company only until 1821. After 1846 Samuel Kirk was joined variously by his three sons. Together they produced elegant silver in the Rococo taste, although they are best known for introducing their repoussé technique to the USA and creating silver embossed with floral, chinoiserie, or architectural ornament. In 1979 the firm merged with the Stieff Co.; it is now known as the Kirk Stieff Co.

▲ ROCOCO REVIVAL Highly decorative and of fine craftsmanship, this desirable vegetable dish (1903–24), which is one of a pair by S. Kirk & Son, is lavishly embossed and chased with whimsical landscapes and romantic figures in the Rococo-revival style popular from the mid-19thC. Pieces by Kirk can be distinguished in date from variance in the maker's marks. $3,200–4,000 (for a pair)

◀ CHARLES BOYTON As functional items such as this entrée dish were intended to serve a specific purpose, their basic form has remained static and the variety of design is limited. The value of pieces such as this is really determined by either the quality of the design or the decorative techniques employed by individual makers. The desirability of silver wares by the Arts and Crafts designers Charles Boyton and Omar Ramsden, who rejected machine-made decoration, is greatly enhanced by the use of hand techniques and such decoration as chasing. This silver-and-ivory example (1934) by Boyton features casting and hand-hammering on the cover and handles. $1,600–2,400

ART DECO STYLE

- **Period** c.1918–1940
- **Characteristics** bold, geometric forms; angular, architectural outlines
- **Influences** Cubism, Futurism, African Art

▶ ART DECO This French vegetable dish (c.1935) is typically Art Deco. Its form is derived from the French *écuelle*, which was usually circular with two flattened handles and a low domed cover. Top makers such as Bointaburet, Cartier, Cardheillac, and Puiforcat made similar items in the Art Deco period; these fetch a premium. $800–1,120

SOUP TUREENS

From the early 18thC soup was served as part of the first course, alongside boiled meats, fish, and vegetables. As soup was served to guests at the table with great ceremony, the soup tureen became a vehicle for the display of wealth; it was often the most opulent and highly prized piece in the dinner service and was frequently made to commission. Most soup tureens are oval-shaped and of heavy-gauge, lavishly ornamented silver. From the 1730s some exceptionally extravagant soup tureens were crafted by such master silversmiths as Paul de Lamerie, Juste-Aurèle Meissonnier, and Thomas Germain, and these are among the most celebrated items of influential Rococo silver. By the mid-18thC tureens were made with matching stands and ladles and sometimes also with liners. In the Neo-classical period, when the classically-inspired forms for dining-room furnishings by such designers as Robert Adam (1728–92) became influential, simple boat-shaped soup tureens came into vogue, but by the early 19thC sumptuous designs were popular again. In general soup tureens are extremely valuable – those made before the mid-18thC or by a major maker are especially rare and valuable.

PAUL DE LAMERIE SOUP TUREEN

Paul de Lamerie (1688–1751) is probably the most important 18thC London silversmith. Born in Holland and of Huguenot descent, he moved to London in 1689, where he became apprentice to the Huguenot silversmith Pierre Platel. His early work was in the understated Queen Anne style, but by the 1730s he was the most lauded exponent of the Rococo style. His work includes this magnificent soup tureen, which is of innovative design and unsurpassed craftsmanship. Realistically modelled as a turtle with a small turtle finial, it is a rare masterpiece and was probably copied directly from a live model in the workshop.
De Lamerie registered several marks including the two shown here.
$1,200,000–1,600,000

▼ MID-18THC SOUP TUREENS

The earliest mid-18thC soup tureens were commonly oval-shaped with decorative cast side handles and domed covers, with finials, perhaps cast as an artichoke, a crayfish, or a simple knop. As exemplified by this fine soup tureen of 1746, they usually stand on four cast feet, and are often fitted with detachable drop-in liners of thin sheet silver, or later of Sheffield plate, that were easy to clean. Most early tureens are of heavy-gauge silver and feature engraved coats-of-arms. Tureen covers and stands have often been lost and then replaced in the more fashionable style-of-the-moment, so original examples are rare. Soup tureens are prone to wear and damage and are costly to repair, especially when worn thin.
$8,000–11,200

◀ BOAT-SHAPED SOUP TUREENS
Boat-shaped soup tureens were in vogue in the Neo-classical period. Most are oval (vase form) on single pedestal feet, with domed covers, high loop handles, and urn-shaped finials. Produced in the 1790s from a minimum amount of sheet silver, this soup tureen is consequently very light and less resistant to damage than examples made in the early 18thC. $4,800–8,000

▶ AMERICAN SOUP TUREENS
This late Federal soup tureen (*c.*1820) by Baldwin Gardiner of New York owes its form to that of the ancient "Warwick" vase. Although the casting and chasing are of very fine quality and the stand is still present – this adds to the value – the proportions are rather clumsy, and the decoration is almost too elaborate to be pleasing. It is a good example of how silversmiths in the USA did not always succeed in adopting and reinterpreting styles. $32,000–56,000

◀ SIMPLICITY OF FORM
This tureen (1870s) by Christopher Dresser has an insulated finial and handles, which make it easier to use without burning the hands. Such practical points formed the cornerstone of Dresser's design ethic of simplicity, purity of form and minimal decoration. $6,400–8,000

▶ COMMISSIONS
From the 19thC colossal soup tureens made in an earlier style were commissioned by royalty and the nobility throughout Europe. A massive tureen such as this German example of 1904 (one of a pair) was intended to display the status of the owner, and usually formed part of a dinner service that also included mirrored *plateaux* and huge silver candelabra. $48,000–64,000 (for a single)

SAUCEBOATS, ARGYLLS & SAUCE TUREENS

Sauceboats, which were introduced in the reign of George I (1714–27), were used for serving gravy or the rich sauces that accompanied fish and meat dishes. Most were made in pairs, or sets of four or six for larger services. Early sauceboats had shallow boat-shaped bodies and were plain, with only gadrooned rims and engraved crests or coats-of-arms for decoration. Mid-18thC examples had deeper bodies with three shell feet. Decoration was still minimal, although a few ornate Rococo examples exist.

After a hiatus in the Regency period, sauceboats were again popular with the Victorians, although generally in 18thC-revival styles. Argylls – produced in the second half of the 18thC – are typically in the shape of small coffeepots, with internal devices for keeping the gravy hot. Covered sauce tureens became fashionable in the 1770s, as they were better suited to keeping sauces hot than open sauceboats. Some had matching ladles and stands, which protected the table from the heat.

► **EARLY SAUCEBOATS**
This fine George II boat-shaped sauceboat is one of a pair that is fairly typical of those made in the 1730s. The "halo" around the crest shows a difference in surface patina and suggests that an earlier crest has been removed, which will affect the value if the silver has become very thin. $1,280–1,920 ($4,800+ for a pair)

◄ **ELABORATE SAUCEBOATS**
Double-lipped sauceboats such as this rare, extremely expensive gem – one of a pair (1732) by the celebrated silversmith Paul de Lamerie – were introduced to England from France c.1717. They are generally of superb quality and attractive, and hence exceptionally desirable. $112,000–160,000 (for a good-quality pair)

► **HELMET-SHAPED SAUCEBOATS**
Helmet-shaped sauceboats with deep bowls and accentuated spouts became popular in the 1760s. This fine example of 1764 is heavy, and a set of four would be fairly valuable. $11,200–16,000 (for a set of four)

ARGYLLS

Argylls are small vessels, designed to keep gravy warm by means of a hot iron, water jacket, or burner, and were more efficient at this than sauceboats.

They were made in a variety of shapes and sizes, but most resemble the form of a covered coffeepot with a handle and spout. Supposedly conceived in the mid-18thC by one of the

Dukes of Argyll who disliked cold gravy, they were produced until the Victorian period in both silver and Sheffield plate. Argylls are quite rare and very collectible. $3,200–4,800

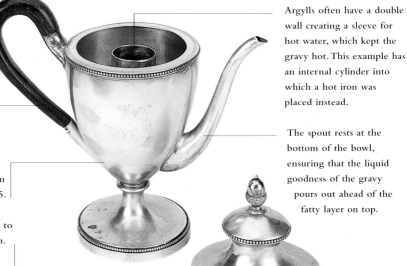

Argylls often have a double wall creating a sleeve for hot water, which kept the gravy hot. This example has an internal cylinder into which a hot iron was placed instead.

The insulated handle prevents the hands from burning.

The vase shape of this example, with delicate beaded borders, was common from 1785 until 1795.

The cover also helps to keep the gravy warm.

The spout rests at the bottom of the bowl, ensuring that the liquid goodness of the gravy pours out ahead of the fatty layer on top.

◀ **SAUCE TUREENS**

Sauce tureens are usually similar in design to soup tureens but smaller. This example, made in 1775 by Makepeace & Carter, is in the Neo-classical style; if it had been copied from a traceable design

by Robert Adam, its value would be significantly increased. It has cast swags and is quite heavy in weight. Cast decoration – cast borders, finial, foot, ram's mask handles, festoons, and paterae – add to the weight and value. $4,800–8,000 (for a pair)

▶ **BOAT-SHAPED SAUCE TUREENS**

The boat shape used on this example of 1791 by Robert Sharp was a popular form for sauce tureens from the late 18thC. Most are sold in pairs or multiples and as such command a premium. Check that covers match and fit, and bear the same marks as the base. $3,200–6,400 (for a pair)

WAITERS, SALVERS & TAZZE

From the mid-17thC salvers were used to serve food and drink, or as stands for porringers and caudle cups. Most salvers are circular or oval shaped, and the finest ones were gilded and decorated with chased-and-engraved ornament. Small salvers, typically measuring 6in (15cm) in diameter, are known as "waiters". They were used not for serving food but for presenting calling cards or messages. A salver on a stemmed foot is sometimes called a tazza. The earliest tazze were made of thin-gauge metal with a central trumpet-shaped foot that was sometimes detachable; however, in the reign of George I (1714–27) this trumpet-shaped foot was replaced by three or four small cast feet.

◀ WAITERS

Owing to their small size, waiters such as this fine George II example (1752) by the London maker Robert Abercromby, who specialized in them, were usually made in pairs. They have feet, most commonly of hoof, scroll, or pad form, which are delicate and prone to damage. The center of a waiter should be checked to ensure that it has not been over-polished where an original crest has been removed, as this will leave the silver thin. $1,920–2,880 (for a pair)

▶ SQUARE WAITERS

This good-quality but affordable Edwardian waiter has been modeled after the square salvers popular in the 1730s. By this period waiters were not made solely for calling cards, but were put to a variety of other practical uses, such as stands for cruet sets. $160–240

◀ AMERICAN SALVERS

Silver made in North America before the War of Independence (1775–83) is very rare and sought after. Salvers made at this period tend to be round – most salvers made after the Revolution are oval. This example (1767) by the Boston maker Paul Revere (1735–1818) is simply engraved with an initial – other examples, especially later ones, typically feature more elaborate engraving. $40,000–56,000

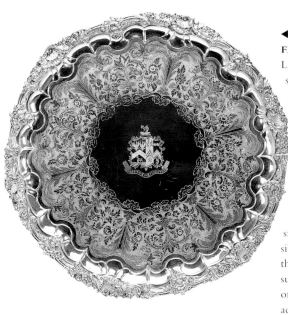

◀ ELABORATE FLAT CHASING
Large decorative salvers often graced sideboards as displays of wealth and status. Massive, heavily decorated examples such as this were made in large numbers between the 1820s and 1840s by top silversmiths. On this silver example (1833) the decoration surrounding the coat-of-arms has been achieved by flat chasing – a technique in which the metal is displaced by a blunt-ended tool but not removed. In the mid-19thC flat-chased decoration was sometimes applied to vessels of an earlier date, but the decoration of this impressive salver is contemporary with its manufacture and this enhances the value. Many fine salvers feature flat-chased decoration depicting wildlife, flora and fauna, or architectural scenes. $8,000–11,200

▶ SILVER-GILT TAZZA
Salvers supported on stem feet, such as this example were used for serving drinks and often known as tazze. Early 18thC examples usually have cast feet and are more solidly made than their late 17thC counterparts. They should be marked on both the flat top sections and on the feet. $8,000–11,200

◀ TAZZA BY JENSEN
There are several types of tazza – some were used as drinking cups, some for serving drinks and others for holding delicacies. Known as a "bon bon tazza", this small (7in/17.5cm) footed sweetmeat dish (*c.*1925), made in the "Grape" design by the Danish silversmith Georg Jensen, has been cast with clusters of fruit on a swirling lobed pedestal. The high quality of the hand-hammered work and cast decoration enhance its desirability. Early 20thC vessels by Jensen are even more desirable than his later work. Look out for the initials of specific designers stamped next to the marks, as these add considerable value. $2,880–3,520

FLATWARE I

Before the custom of setting a table with flatware was introduced in the 17thC, spoons and knives were numbered among personal possessions. Spoons, used since before Roman times, survive in great quantities and are among the most collectible items of utilitarian silver. By far the most personal of all pieces of silver from medieval times, they were given as baptism presents and were carried throughout life. Being "born with a silver spoon in your mouth" carried great social significance, as wealth and status determined the quality of one's spoon. Food was eaten with a spoon until the 16thC, when the fork – until then used only for desserts and sweetmeats – began to be taken up in continental Europe as the utensil of choice. The fashion for eating with a fork was adopted by the court of Charles II while in exile in France and brought to England after the Restoration of the Monarchy in 1660. From the early 18thC sets of matching spoons, forks, and knives were made in a vast range of patterns.

▶ TREFID SPOONS

Fashions from France influenced flatware styles from the mid-17thC. New styles included "trefid" spoons with egg-shaped bowls, broad flat stems ending in a trefoil (sometimes notched), and tapering ribs, or "rats' tails", at the junction of bowl and stem for extra stength. As on these silver-gilt examples (c.1700) by the Plymouth silversmith John Murch, they were often stamped or engraved with decorative scrolls, foliage or beading. $1,600–2,400 (for a pair)

▼ CUTLERY BOXES

Usually of mahogany, or covered with leather, velvet, shagreen, or wood veneers with silver trims, ornamental boxes for holding sets of silver cutlery came into fashion in the reign of George II (1727–60). Often designed as a pair to stand at each end of a sideboard, they were typically of square form with a sloping bombé front. Rarely found today with their original contents or interiors, these boxes are often used by collectors as stationery or decanter boxes. $800–1,600

◀ FORKS

The earliest English dining forks date from the mid-17thC and had two or three tines. They were set following the French custom with the open "bowl" facing the table, which is why original engraving usually appears on the stem back. Early forks in good condition are very rare, especially dessert forks. Beware of fakes created by soldering modern forks onto the stems of old spoons. Four-pronged forks were introduced in the 1720s and were commonplace from the 1760s. $160–320 (each)

▶ **SERVING SPOONS**
Serving spoons, which are
of medium-large size (length
12¾-14¼in/33–38cm) were first
used in the mid-17thC, but they
became more commonplace
from the 1700s. This example
of 1740 is in the Hanoverian
pattern. $1,600–2,400

◀ **BERRY SPOONS**
Berry spoons are used for serving
fruit; most are made in pairs or
sets of four and six and are sold
in velvet-lined cases. Typically, this
example is a George III tablespoon
(1780), later decorated – probably
during the Victorian era – with
embossed fruit. $50+ (each)

▶ **TODDY LADLES**
Toddy ladles, made primarily
in Scotland and Ireland, similar
to sauce ladles but with longer,
slimmer stems and small, shallow
bowls, were used to serve hot
toddy from a punchbowl. Sets of
six (typical) and provincial ladles
are most desirable. $80–480

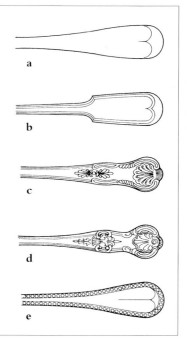

STYLES OF FLATWARE
a) "Old English"
This simple pattern, where the handle remains undecorated
and the terminal features a central inward point, or "pip", was
made from *c*.1760. It is a derivative of the Hanoverian pattern.
b) "Fiddle"
Used in Britain from *c*.1820, the "Fiddle" pattern is so called
because the shape of the handle resembles that of a violin.
c) "King's"
This elaborate pattern with waisted sides features a scallop
shell and anthemion motifs and was particularly popular
during the Regency period (*c*.1790–1820).
d) "Queen's"
Similar to the "King's" pattern, although even more elaborate,
with a convex shell motif, the "Queen's" pattern was first
used from *c*.1820.
e) "Beaded"
Flatware embellished with a continuous border of beaded
decoration was especially popular in the Victorian period.
The pattern was copied from a late 18thC beaded design (rare).

FLATWARE II

The fashion for knives, forks, and spoons made as matching sets was first sparked off in England in the early 18thC. (Sets or part sets of spoons and forks from the 17thC and earlier do exist, but they are very rare.) The "Hanoverian" pattern was the first one used for matching flatware; it evolved into the "Old English" pattern in the 1760s. From the late 18thC flatware was produced in services in a variety of patterns, elaborate silver-gilt dessert services became fashionable, in keeping with the trend for lavish dining customs. Of major influence on flatware design and production was the launch from the 1770s of mechanized silver manufacturing, notably in Sheffield, which became the main centre for cutlery production in England. The most popular late 18th and early 19thC flatware designs include the "Fiddle" pattern and the lavishly decorated "King's" and "Queen's" patterns. It is rare to find a complete, original set of flatware, as pieces were often replaced after heavy use. Other items of flatware include fish slices and pretty boxed sets of matching coffee spoons.

◀ **PLACE SETTING**
Although this complete Victorian "King's" pattern place setting includes 1930s knives with stainless steel blades, today these are preferable to the worn original steel blades. Flatware services in sets of twelve and more pieces are considerably more desirable and valuable than those of six, especially if in good condition and original. $6,400–9,600 (for 12 place settings)

▶ **AMERICAN PATTERNS**
Whereas in England the same pattern could be used by many makers, in the USA patterns were patented and used only by one manufacturer. The date when the pattern was patented is often stamped on the back of the stem. This silver-gilt part service (c.1900) by Tiffany & Co. features the "Richelieu" pattern. Part services by such a reputable firm as Tiffany can usually be added to in order to build up a complete service; however, this is often difficult with flatware by more minor makers. $7,200–8,800 (for a part service of 12 pieces)

◄ **MODERN DESIGNS**
This Danish "Caravel" place setting (c.1960), designed by Henning Koppel and produced by Georg Jensen, is superbly crafted. Any number of matching specialist utensils, including soup ladles, basting spoons, fish knives, and fruit forks, can still be ordered today to augment a setting such as this. $4,800–5,600 (for a 13-piece place setting)

► **FISH KNIFE AND FORK**
This solidly made Edwardian fish knife and fork (1904) have ivory handles that have begun to part company with the delicately engraved silver – probably due to frequent exposure to hot water during cleaning. Both ivory and mother-of-pearl were often used for the handles of dessert or fish knives and forks, and these should always be examined for signs of weakness or damage through regular use. Sets of serving utensils may be found fitted in silk- or velvet-lined boxes, and if in good condition they will fetch a high price. Although this fish knife and its companion fork are attractive, their value is substantially diminished because of the poor condition. $95–160

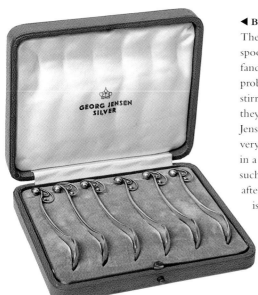

◄ **BOXED SETS**
These stylish "Magnolia" design spoons (c.1925), decorated with fanciful berry terminals, were probably meant to be used for stirring tea or coffee. Although they were made by Georg Jensen, they would be worth very little individually. However, in a well-presented labeled box such as this one, they are sought after by collectors and the value is considerably increased. Pieces from the early 20thC are more sought after than late 20thC examples, and will fetch a higher price. $800–1,280

CONDIMENTS I

The range of small silver items associated with the flavoring of food – common, to prevent it (especially meat) from spoiling or to disguise unpalatable flavours – expanded significantly during the 18thC. These items included a number of novel forms, such as cruet stands, introduced to England from France by immigrant Huguenot silversmiths. Other traditional kinds of plate such as pepper casters were reinterpreted or refined according to the latest fashions. Under the influence of the French court, dining customs had become more elaborate, and small, predominantly utilitarian accessories came to form an essential part of the table setting. Unlike more elaborate items such as centrepieces, tureens, and salvers, these everyday necessities were not designed to impress. They were made in great numbers in a variety of decorative styles, and today comprise an important collecting area.

▶ WARWICK CRUETS

Cruet stands, fitted with an assortment of silver and glass bottles and casters, were first produced in the early 18thC. Early examples were designed to hold oil and vinegar only, while larger stands, common by the 1720s, also held salt, pepper, and mustard. This cinquefoil frame featuring a central scroll handle is often known as a "Warwick" cruet, after a fine example of 1715 by Anthony Nelme that was once in the collection of Warwick Castle, Warwickshire. This was a popular mid-18thC design, and many such cruets were produced by Samuel Wood – a specialist cruet and caster maker. On this example of 1749 a cartouche has been soldered between the guard rings and base for engraving a crest. Collectors should check that the bottle covers and casters are all matching and fully marked. The stand base should also be fully hallmarked. $6,400–9,600

◀ SOY FRAMES

Smaller versions of cruet stands, made from the 1760s to hold four to eight small bottles of sauces and condiments, are known as soy frames. As on this example (1772), most had wooden bases with pierced sides, similar in form to wine coasters. By the end of the 18thC cruet stands and soy frames were made larger to hold as many as ten bottles. Miniature versions of wine labels, engraved with the names of sauces, would have hung around the necks of the bottles, and these are very sought after by collectors today, especially those with unusual names such as Catsup, Anchovie Chile or Vinaigrette. $640–960

COLLECTING

● Soy frames were often poorly constructed of thin sheet metal, so few survive in good condition.
● The covers of pepper boxes should be original and fit snugly.
● Condiment sets in good condition are extremely rare. A complete set is much more valuable than a single caster.
● Watch out for mustard pots that have been converted from small mugs by the addition of a cover. Also avoid damaged mustard pots.

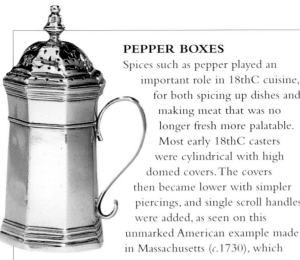

PEPPER BOXES

Spices such as pepper played an important role in 18thC cuisine, for both spicing up dishes and making meat that was no longer fresh more palatable. Most early 18thC casters were cylindrical with high domed covers. The covers then became lower with simpler piercings, and single scroll handles were added, as seen on this unmarked American example made in Massachusetts (c.1730), which was known in the USA as a "pepper box". Long-necked examples with slightly baluster-shaped bodies were popular c.1735. By 1730 casters no longer had handles and the pear shape was the most typical. The finials and handles are most prone to wear and may have been replaced. Watch out for "marriages" of a body and a cover; a difference in the color of the patina of the two parts is usually a good indication that they have been married. $2,880–3,840

► VICTORIAN NOVELTIES

The Victorians were extremely fond of such novelty forms as these amusing animal-shaped casters. The "dog" is probably Toby – the companion of the characters Mr and Mrs Punch – who was often made as part of a condiment set, with Mr Punch as the mustard pot and Mrs Punch and Toby as salt and pepper casters. This example is heavily constructed, having been cast in solid silver, but the bear on the right is of a much lighter construction. A leading maker of novelty condiment sets and salts was the London-based Hennells family, whose work as silversmiths spanned five generations. Novelty-shaped mustard pots are also extremely popular among collectors today. $1,280–1,920 (each)

◄ MUSTARD POTS

Until the mid-18thC mustard was a dry condiment that was served from unpierced ("blind") casters and prepared on the plate. From the 1760s pots for paste mustard came into fashion and were made in a range of sizes and designs. This example (1843) is in the form of a tankard – the basic shape of the earliest mid-18thC mustard pots. It features a blue-glass liner to prevent the silver from being corroded by the acidic vinegar in the mustard. Mustard spoons have drop-shaped bowls, as opposed to salt spoons with round or oval bowls, and slightly shorter stems. The accompanying silver mustard spoon features a slightly curved stem and deep elongated bowl for serving the mustard easily from the pot. Beware of pots that have been converted from small mugs by the addition of a cover. $400–480

CONDIMENTS II

Salt cellars (or salts) are among the most varied and attractive small items of silver. From the late 17thC the most popular type of salt cellar, usually made in pairs or sets, was the trencher salt, of circular, octagonal or triangular form, with a central well. By the 1730s this style has been superseded by the circular cauldron salt cellar on three feet. Many cauldron salts, especially those made between the 1750s and 1780s, were inexpensively, and therefore lightly, constructed and are prone to damage. Condition is vital with salt cellars – the corrosive nature of salt, particularly when damp, means that many salts are corroded or stained with black spots, which reduces the value. Fine-quality 20thC condiment sets signed by a renowned craftsman are very desirable, especially if sold in the original cases.

◀ LAVISH SALTS
This large, elaborate salt (1815), which is one of a set of eight by the London maker Paul Storr, has been lavishly decorated with heavy cast ornament, which adds to the weight and, combined with the importance of the silversmith, makes this piece extremely valuable. Avoid both salts with retouched decoration and plain 18thC examples with later embossing. $32,000–48,000 (for a set of eight)

▶ NAUTICAL THEMES
This highly elaborate parcel-gilt salt is one of a pair made in 1850 by the celebrated French firm of silversmiths, Messrs Odiot. To tie in with its purpose of containing salt, it has a nautical theme, with the bowl in the shape of a shell and the stem decorated with stylized dolphins. $2,400–3,200

◀ OMAR RAMSDEN
One of a pair, this basin-shaped salt (1920) made by Omar Ramsden has been hand-hammered and decorated with applied borders and pierced work. The bowl is supported on cast, buttress-like openwork feet reminiscent of medieval designs. Silver by Ramsden that is marked and inscribed "Omar Ramsden me fecit" (literally, "Omar Ramsden made me") is valuable, and this fine salt would be a good investment. $960–1,280 (for a pair)

▲ FRENCH SALTS
In the late 19thC it became fashionable to set each place at the table with small individual condiment holders or sets. This French salt dish from the 1880s/1890s would originally have been part of a set with matching spoons. These sets, which were sometimes equipped with glass liners, were often fitted in leather presentation boxes and were popularly given as wedding gifts. $320–640 (for a boxed set of four)

CHARLES BOYTON MARK
This mark demonstrates the following:
Maker's facsimile signature
CB   Maker's mark for
                           Charles Boyton
Lion Passant   Sterling silver
                           (standard mark)
Leopard's Head Assay mark
                           for London
Date Mark   "U" for 1935
Double profile Commemorative mark;
                           Golden Jubilee of
                           George V and
                           Queen Mary

◀ HANDMADE SETS
This set (1934) by the highly respected London maker Charles Boyton comprises pots for pepper, salt and mustard, with two matching spoons. The bowls have been raised by hand and deftly spot-hammered for a fine, delicate finish. These hand-crafted sets were often commissioned, and in such instances a family crest, monogram, or armorial may have been incorporated into the design. The emblems cannot easily be removed, and in most cases they will detract from rather than increase the value. $800–1,600

▶ 1960S DESIGN
Although stylish and extremely well made, such condiment sets as this 1960s example by Georg Jensen are not yet always embraced by popular taste. Collectors should buy them as an investment with caution. $1,920–2,400

EPERGNES & CENTERPIECES

Epergnes and centerpieces are among the many items of large, richly decorated tableware intended primarily to reflect the wealth and status of their owner. Epergnes were first used as extravagant centrepieces at the French court in the late 17thC. Comprising a single stand with a central basket surrounded by several small bowls, the épergne was introduced to England *c.*1715 and most popular in the mid-18thC. Early examples featured candle sockets, which if necessary could be exchanged for smaller baskets. By the 1740s épergnes were most usually associated with the dessert course and used to hold fruits, candied fruits, and sweetmeats. In the early 19thC ornamental centerpieces with central bowls for candied fruits and sweetmeats, either made of solid silver or pierced with a glass liner, replaced épergnes as the decorative focal point of the dining-table. As centerpieces were so valuable, many were fitted in wooden boxes with baize linings to protect them when not in use. Decorative centerpieces were often used as presentation items, especially during the Regency period.

◀ **EPERGNES**
This extremely fine George III épergne (1771) by the leading silversmith Thomas Pitts can be made smaller by removing the top layer of branches and using the bowls for bon-bon dishes and the larger central dish as a fruit basket. Holes that were left when the detachable scroll branches and baskets were removed for cleaning were disguised with silver caps, usually in the form of flower bosses. $24,000–32,000

▶ **REGENCY CENTERPIECES**
In the Regency period (*c.*1790–1820) heavy stands with scroll feet and female caryatid figures supporting the central bowl were very popular. At this time centerpieces assumed a new role as gifts or prizes for historic or sporting events. This fine example by Paul Storr (1771–1844) has been inscribed at a later date for an automobile rally in Monte Carlo. Later inscriptions do generally diminish the value of a piece. In spite of this, the highly skilled modeling of the figures and the reputation of the maker make this a sought-after piece. $12,800–19,200

COLLECTING
● Delicate branches, feet and pierced decoration are prone to damage, so check carefully for repairs.
● The body and central basket of an épergne should be fully hallmarked, with other parts at least stamped with a maker's mark and the lion passant. Unmarked baskets or bowls may be replacements.

► CONDITION

This old Sheffield plate centerpiece with glass bowls has its origins in the épergne, although épergnes featured silver bowls. If the glass bowls are later replacements, or chipped or cracked, this will dramatically reduce the value. Also make sure that, on areas that have been frequently polished, such as the ornate scrolled feet, the plate has not worn off, leaving the copper base (revealed as pink) showing through.
$2,400–3,200

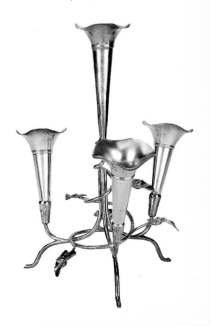

◄ ELECTROPLATE

By the second half of the 19thC the form of centerpieces had changed dramatically, mainly due to the Birmingham firm of Elkington & Co., which pioneered a method of electroplating that made it possible to produce such elaborate items more affordably. The highly innovative one-off designs shown at the Great Exhibition of 1851 inspired manufacturers to make wildly imaginative forms such as this large centerpiece with applied palm fronds and matching dessert stand. $3,200–4,800

▼ LATER DESIGNS

By the end of the 19thC centerpieces such as this elegant plated example (c.1899), which features a large central vase for flowers and three smaller bud vases, had become smaller and less elaborate. The attenuated form of the trumpet vases is highly typical of the Art Nouveau style. $160–320

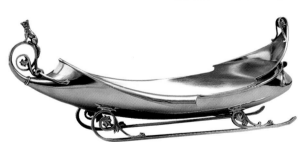

▲ QUIRKY FORMS

Made by the American firm of Gorham & Co., of Providence, Rhode Island, this silver-gilt centerpiece in the form of a sled (c.1890) is characteristic of the 19thC taste for novelty forms, which were especially popular among the Victorians. The fashionable Art Nouveau style of the period is reflected in the graceful curving boat shape of the sled and the delicate openwork tendrils on the runners and handles.
$1,920–2,880

BASKETS & BOWLS

Silver-handled baskets, which were placed in the center of the dining table for serving sweetmeats, bread, fruit, or cake, were rare before the second quarter of the 18thC. The earliest examples were of oval shape, with pierced and chased sides simulating wicker work, and flat bases, which were usually decorated with coats-of-arms. Until the 1720s, a handle was placed at each end of the basket, but by the mid-18thC hinged central swing handles had become standard. The body of a basket was normally constructed from a single piece of silver, which was hammered up to form a bowl; cast ornament, a cast foot, and a handle were then added. With increased mass-production from the 1770s, baskets were made from thin sheets of stamped silver, which resulted in poorer quality, lighter, easily damaged designs. Bowls, which in contrast to baskets do not have handles, have long been produced in a great variety of decorative forms and designs for many different purposes. Their decorative and functional appeal ensures that they remain popular among collectors today.

▶ NEO-CLASSICAL BASKETS

Towards the end of the Neo-classical period, the most popular baskets were oval or boat-shaped on a raised foot. Most were decorated with applied Classical ornament, with reeded borders or beaded work around the rim. Pierced work, seen on this example of 1802 by William Frisbee, was a favoured technique at this time, but it should be checked carefully for signs of damage or repair. Some of the finest 18thC baskets were made by such silversmiths as Paul de Lamerie, William Plummer, and Burradge Davenport. Early baskets should be marked underneath. A good place to look for the marks on baskets such as this example is along the rim where the handle meets the body. On examples such as this featuring pierced decoration, the marks are often lost in the pierced work. Handles should always be at least partly marked. $3,200–4,800

PAUL STORR

Paul Storr (1771–1844), who is closely associated with the London firm of Rundell, Bridge & Rundell for whom he produced much fine silver, is probably the most acclaimed Regency silversmith. One of his later marks – "P.S" within an outline of two conjoined circles) is shown.

P·S

◀ WIREWORK BASKETS

In the last 20 years of the 18thC it was discovered that silver could be successfully drawn into wires and used to imaginative visual effect. Wirework was an ideal technique to use on such items as this fine design of 1817 by Paul Storr, which simulates the open lattice weave of a basket. The form is fairly unusual for its time. $16,000–19,200

◀ DECORATIVE MOTIFS
The decorative motifs that embellished baskets such as this example (1838) by H. Wilkinson & Co. of Sheffield often provide a clue as to the basket's intended use – for example, sheaves of wheat for bread or bunches of grapes for fruit. Reproductions of 18thC basket forms, especially Neo-classical boat shapes, were also popular at this period. $1,120–1,600

▶ ART NOUVEAU
This bread basket (1905) by William Haseler of Birmingham has been stamped out from a disc of silver with the sides pierced using a mechanized press. It is finely designed in the Art Nouveau style, with characteristic colored enameling. $5,600–6,400

◀ MUFFIN DISH & COVER
This Arts and Crafts style muffin dish of exceptional quality was made by Charles Robert Ashbee (1863–1942). Muffin dishes were commonly made in silver plate from the late Victorian period until the 1930s, and these more modest examples can be bought at very reasonable prices. $6,400–8,000

▶ ART DECO
Made in France by the firm of Christofle, this elegant Art Deco fruit bowl (c.1930) is typical of the style with its clean lines and minimal decoration. Similar ivory-and-silver bowls were made in England by Viners of Sheffield. $3,520–4,000

MISCELLANEOUS I

The table was the center of social activity in the 17th and 18thC, and formal dining encouraged the use of many dining accessories. Notable implements include meat skewers, which were first made in silver from the mid-18thC, when it was fashionable for the hostess to carve meat at the table; marrow scoops for extracting marrow jelly from bones; scissors for selecting grapes from a bunch; egg frames for serving eggs; and toast racks. When extensive mechanized production was introduced in the 19thC, a great assortment of dining silver was manufactured in vast quantities, making miscellaneous items such as these widely available to the collector today.

◀ MEAT SKEWERS

The earliest silver meat skewers seem to date from the mid-18thC. As on this example of 1793, most have a ring at one end to facilitate withdrawal or to hang on a hook, although some skewers have decorative terminals. Sometimes they were made in graduated sets and decorated to match flatware patterns. Meat skewers were very rarely used by the 1850s, and today are often seen used as paper knives. $160–320

▶ MARROW SPOONS AND SCOOPS

Roasted marrow bones were a popular snack in England from the 17thC until the Victorian period, and in the early 18thC long implements were devised to facilitate the removal of the jelly, which was a great delicacy and highly nutritious. Marrow spoons (near right, *c.*1770) have conventional bowls at one end for eating stew and thin scoops at the other end for extracting the marrow when the bones were brought to the table. Marrow scoops (far right, 1762) are a variation on marrow spoons, but are thinner and usually have one or two channelled ends for marrow of different widths. Marrow spoon $400–480; marrow scoop $160–190

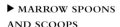

POULTRY SKEWERS

Smaller versions of meat skewers – some examples measuring only 3in (7.5cm) in length – were made for poultry. Produced mainly in continental Europe, early (pre-1770) poultry skewers are rare and extremely collectible, as are those featuring cast heraldic terminals.

◀ GRAPE SCISSORS

Grape scissors with inset steel blades were used for cutting grapes from a bunch. The earliest scissors from the late 18thC are simple and elegant, while those made in the Regency and Victorian periods tend to be lavishly decorated with trailing vines. Sometimes they formed part of a large dessert set, along with nutcrackers and toothpicks. As grape scissors such as this pair of 1840 make ideal gifts, they are highly sought after and achieve high prices, and those found with their original fitted cases are especially desirable. Check for damaged pivots and loose mechanisms, as these are expensive to repair. $400–480

▶ EGG FRAMES

From the early 18thC until the Edwardian period, eggs were commonly brought to the table in cruets, or egg frames, which were fitted with detachable cups and spoons that were usually parcel gilded to protect the silver from staining caused by the sulphur present in eggs, as in this example of 1796. Elaborate versions were fitted with salt cellars, and in the early 19thC individual frames were made combining one or two egg cups with salt and pepper pots and a small toast rack. $1,120–1,600

◀ TOAST RACKS

The earliest toast racks date from the mid-18thC and were simply fashioned from silver wire, as seen in this large example of 1847, which is topped by a heart-shaped handle. In the Regency period heavier, elaborately decorated examples were favored, and in the Victorian period novelty forms were popular. $400–640

▶ VICTORIAN NOVELTIES

This toast rack (1896), standing on four ball feet with wishbone-shaped bars, is an example of a serviceable novelty of which the Victorians were particularly fond. Toast racks such as this are inexpensively constructed from wire that has been bent and soldered; they are often small and found in pairs. Toast racks were made in great quantities in old Sheffield plate and electroplate. Look out for expanding concertina-style examples. $160–200

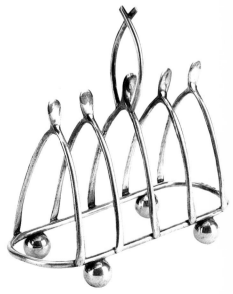

MISCELLANEOUS II

The items featured here – dish rings, card holders, honey skeps, and strawberry dishes – cover just some of the hugely diverse range of miscellaneous dining silver available to collectors. Dish rings were made exclusively in Ireland from the mid-18thC; they are typically decorated with intricate piercing and are avidly collected. Also desirable are small decorative holders for menu or place cards, which were popularly used at formal dinners from the late 19thC. Both are similar in design, although place-card holders are generally smaller than those for menu cards. Honey skeps, which are usually made in the forms of beehives in honey-colored silver gilt, are more rare but still very sought after; examples by known makers can reach a premium. "Strawberry" dish is a term for a shallow circular dish with a fluted edge, made from the late 17thC and often gilded; however, the name is misleading, as these dishes were used not only for strawberries but also for all types of dessert.

▲ DISH RINGS

Dish rings, which are sometimes erroneously called "potato" rings, were used to raise dishes off the surface of a polished wooden table – an Irish speciality from the mid-18thC. The finest versions are pierced and embossed with Rococo ornament of birds, farm animals, rustic figures, foliage, architecture, and sometimes an engraved coat-of-arms. Many dish rings, such as these pierced examples from Dublin, were made in the early 20thC, but these are less sought after than their 18thC counterparts. Most dish rings seem to be fitted with blue-glass liners (as shown on these examples of 1898 and 1912). The liners enable the dish rings to be used to hold fruit or flowers. Examples made in Ireland in the 18thC and provincial Irish examples (even later ones) are very valuable. $1,120–1,600 (each)

IRISH MARKS

From 1637 Irish silver was stamped with an assay mark of a crowned harp to prescribe the sterling standard. The crowned harp was also used as the Dublin town mark between 1637 and 1730, after which time a mark showing the seated figure of Hibernia was employed as well.
In 1638 date letters were introduced for Irish silver; however, they followed a haphazard system and were often omitted altogether.

▶ MENU-CARD HOLDERS

Most menu-card holders are in the disc shape of these silver-and-tortoiseshell Edwardian examples (1904), which as a cased set are desirable. Many examples feature enamel plaques decorated with sporting motifs, animals, game birds (*see* far right), or vintage cars. Cased set $960–1,280; pheasant card holder $320–400

▶ ART NOUVEAU

In 1896 the antiques dealer
Samuel Bing opened a
gallery in Paris that acted as
a forum for the avant-garde
work of designers opposed
to the mechanization of the
mid- to late 19thC. Inspired
by nature, their work is
dominated by asymmetrical
lines, insect motifs, and
ethereal maidens, as on
this menu-card holder
(1902). $640–960 (for
a cased set of six)

ALSO POPULAR:

- apple corers
- asparagus tongs
- dish crosses (two silver
arms crossed in an X
shape over a central
burner, used for keeping
dishes hot at the table)
- nutmeg graters
- spoon trays (used in the
early 18thC, when tea was
drunk from a bowl rather
than a cup with a saucer)

◀ HONEY SKEPS

Designed to imitate early
dome-shaped beehives made
of horizontal coils of tied straw,
honey skeps were made mainly
during the reign of George III
(1760–1820) to contain glass
honey pots. As in this
example of 1803,
honey skeps should
have matching saucer
stands; they are often engraved
on the side of the body with a
flying "bee" – here, the finial is
in the shape of a bee. Many
examples are gilded, of fine
quality and keenly sought after
by collectors for their novelty
value. Here the glass liner for
honey has been lost, although
this will not affect the value.
$4,800–6,400

▶ STRAWBERRY DISHES

From the late 17thC this type
of dish, with an upcurved
scalloped, reeded, and fluted rim,
was a speciality of Huguenot
silversmiths who fled to Britain
and The Netherlands following
the Revocation of the Edict of
Nantes (1685). Made in various
sizes, strawberry dishes are often
undecorated or very simply
engraved with a coat-of-arms or
crest. This large, unusual example,
which is one of a pair produced
in 1815 by the London maker
Robert Garrard, stands on four
scroll feet and is set with nine
Irish agricultural medals.
$8,000–12,800 (for a pair)

The expansion of trade with China, Arabia and the Americas brought tea, coffee and chocolate to Europe in the 17thC. People accustomed to drinking beer, wine, and posset (milk curdled with wine, ale, or vinegar) were captivated by the novelty of these foreign beverages, and as the fashion for drinking them became more widespread, a demand for suitable vessels in which to prepare and serve them was created. Silver pots, kettles, and urns were made, alongside milk jugs, spoons, sugar bowls, and caddies. Widely available in Europe by 1650, tea was expensive and initially the preserve of the upper classes. Coffee was first imported to Europe from the Near East by the Venetians and, being less expensive than tea, became a popular breakfast drink. The sociable nature of this stimulating black liquid sparked the opening of coffee houses across Europe (the first one had opened in London by 1652), and in the second half of the 17thC they were established in most European cities. These coffee houses attracted all classes of society and became important centres for social life and political intrigues. An attempt in 1675 to suppress them as a public nuisance failed, and by 1700 there were more than 400 in London alone. Chocolate was introduced in the late 17thC via trading routes to the West Indies, where it had been known since the discovery of the Americas. Often drunk in coffee houses, chocolate was tiresome to prepare and serve and enjoyed only a brief reputation as a favored drink in fashionable society. By the end of the 18thC tea and coffee wares had become a major part of the silversmith's trade.

TEAPOTS I

The first teapots were not used for brewing tea but for pouring hot water over tea leaves into cups. In the 17thC shapes imitated the tapering cylinder and straight spout of contemporary coffeepots, hexagonal wine pots, or globular porcelain teapots imported from China. Early 18thC teapots were pear-shaped and octagonal, before adopting the bullet form in the 1730s. Most were of heavy-gauge silver, with separately made foot rims, spouts cast in two halves, and minimal surface decoration.

▲ **PEAR SHAPES**
Many early 18thC teapots were pear-shaped, and their small size reflected the high cost of tea. As on this Queen Anne example (1709) by Thomas Parr, spouts were often faceted, sometimes with a hinged flap at the end to retain the heat, although this feature was largely abandoned in the 1720s. Examples in good condition are rare and very valuable. $16,000–24,000

BEWARE
Look carefully at teapots, as many have been heavily used and may have sustained damage. Examine the body for repairs and, if possible, test for leaks. Check hinges, handle sockets, and spouts for splits or signs of wear. Wooden handles are vulnerable to splitting, rotting, and cracking; however, this will not reduce the value, as they can be replaced easily.

BULLET-SHAPED TEAPOTS

The bullet-shaped teapot was a speciality of Scottish silversmiths and fashionable from the 1730s until c.1760. Finials take the form of buds, figures, or birds, and lids are usually flush with the body. The silver handle on this example (1739) by the Edinburgh maker John Main is a feature of Scottish teapots – most English teapots had wooden handles. However, collectors should beware, as bullet teapots are highly prized and often faked today. Some teapots have detachable covers without hinges, and such covers should be at least partly marked. $3,200–4,000

◀ ROCOCO DESIGNS

The inverted pear-shaped teapot, on a short stem with a wide foot rim and a low domed cover, was briefly produced in the 1750s and enjoyed greater popularity in North America than in Britain. This George II example (1753) by Thomas Whipham I is lavishly decorated in typical Rococo style with chased flowers and scrolls, a cast foot, and a pineapple finial. $1,600–2,400

▶ THE TASTE FOR CLASSICISM

The simple vase form, pedestal base, and decorative beading around the body of this teapot, made c.1795 by James Musgrave of Philadelphia, are hallmarks of the taste for Classicism that became fashionable during the latter part of the 18thC and was known in the USA as the Federal style. The severe forms of American tea silver in the Federal style – produced mainly in Boston and Philadelphia – were strongly influenced by English prototypes of more than a decade earlier. However, the elongated proportions and double-domed cover with finial of this example are typically American. $12,800–16,000

TEAPOTS II

Reflecting the influence of the Neo-classical period of the mid-to late 18thC, drum-shaped teapots of plain cylindrical form and oval cylindrical teapots were made from the 1770s. By this date thin-gauge rolled sheet silver had become widely available, making possible the mass-production of silver objects. This innovative method reduced production costs and accommodated new teapot shapes. Cheaper manufacturing costs also sparked the production of matching tea services – although a handful of tea services are known from the early 1700s, the notion of assembling a set of complementary items did not take hold until lower production costs made it feasible in the mid-18thC. In the Regency period (c.1790–1820) low, boat-shaped teapots resembling Classical oil lamps were popular. Most 19thC teapots were created as parts of larger services and were manufactured in a broad range of earlier styles. With the exception of the original Arts and Crafts and Art Deco styles, most 20thC teapots copy or reinterpret earlier designs.

OVAL CYLINDRICAL TEAPOT BY HESTER BATEMAN

The rolled sheet silver used in mass producing silver was well suited to the production of the oval and drum shapes favoured in the late 18thC. As most oval teapots had flat bases, initially many were made with matching stands to protect furniture from the heat of the pot; however, by 1800 most were designed with feet as this was more practical. This example was made in 1780 by Hester Bateman, a leading late 18thC silversmith who expanded her husband's small business following his death in 1760. She was one of the first manufacturers to establish a fully mechanized workshop in London. Tiny versions of this form, for one or two cups, are known as "bachelor", "spinster", or "afternoon" teapots. $640–960

The wooden handle on this piece is typical of earlier teapots; from c.1790 many had ivory handles.

Wooden handles and finials are susceptible to wear, so check that they are not loose and that the sockets are not too damaged, as this would be detrimental to the value.

Sheet-silver teapots are not as sturdy as those raised from heavier-gauge metal and are prone to splitting along the body seams and around the spout.

Hinges are often worn or damaged and are usually costly to repair.

Decoration is normally restricted to beaded, fluted, or reeded rims, as shown on this teapot. Some more valuable examples are decorated with bright-cut engraving of Classically inspired swags, laurel wreaths, and the key pattern.

Although a vast quantity of silver from the Bateman factory survives, much is of very thin gauge and poorly made – the result of mechanized rather than hand-finished production methods.

◀ **REGENCY TEAPOTS**
The drum- and oval-shaped teapots – the latter with straighter sides – popular in the 1790s were succeeded in the early 19thC by the squat, spherical or boat-shaped form exemplified by this teapot by the celebrated silversmith Paul Storr (1771–1844). Made in 1816, this example is heavier and of much better quality than most of its contemporaries and will fetch a high price. $4,000–4,800

▶ **NEO-CLASSICAL REVIVAL STYLE**
The squat vase shape of this teapot and the decorative swags, elaborate beading and leaf ornament emphasize the continuing popularity of the Neo-classical style during the late Victorian period. Teapots were produced in a variety of historical revival styles in the 19thC, and most were made as part of a tea service. A good-quality set will fetch considerably more than the sum of the individual pieces. Made in 1899 by the London firm of Garrard & Co., this example is no longer together with the rest of its set and its value is therefore relatively modest considering the importance of the distinguished maker. $480–560

◀**TEA SERVICES**
A basic tea service consists of a teapot, milk jug and sugar bowl. Added to this might be a hot-water jug, slop bowl, coffeepot, and tray, all with matching decoration. A set with identical marks on each piece is worth far more than a composite service. This five-piece Art Deco silver-and-ivory tea service by Emil Viners of Sheffield (c.1935) is stylish and high quality. $4,800–5,600

TEA-KETTLES

A continuous supply of hot water was needed to replenish small teapots and coffeepots. Tea-kettles were made from the 1730s and were intended to provide boiling water at the table. They were made in two or three parts comprising a kettle, a stand, and a burner, which was occasionally produced separately. Early examples are of circular form and relatively plain. They are usually marked underneath, but the marks have often been rendered illegible by carbon deposits and erosion from the flame of the burner. Tea-kettles waned in popularity after the 1760s, when they were replaced by tea-urns, which were more practical and safer; however, many were made in the mid-Victorian period as parts of tea services. Tea-kettles are no longer used in preparing tea and today are sold purely as decorative items.

▶ ROCOCO-STYLE TEA-KETTLES

This early Victorian tea-kettle is a direct copy of a type produced in the 1740s, when the flamboyant Rococo style was fashionable. The inverted pear-shaped kettle has been lavishly decorated in the finest Rococo tradition, with chased scrolls, flowers, foliage, and shells, and rests on a stand ornamented with a shell-and-foliage-encrusted apron and dolphin-headed scroll feet. Some original Rococo tea-kettles had ivory swing handles similar to this one, although most had metal handles bound in wicker work or covered with a thick leather outer casing to protect the hands from the hot metal. Spirit burners have frequently been lost, so look out for replacements such as the one shown here, which is made of Sheffield plate. If a kettle is still complete with its original stand and burner, all separate parts (including the cover) should bear the same maker's mark. $3,200–4,800

◀ 19THC PRODUCTION

Although after the 1760s tea-kettles were replaced by more practical tea-urns, in the Victorian period tea-kettles such as this ornate example of 1862 were still popularly made as part of tea services in earlier historical styles. This example features a hinged mechanism attaching the kettle to the base, so that the heavy kettle can be tilted forward to fill the teapot more easily. $1,600–2,400

IMPORT MARKS

- Following the Customs Act of 1842 all silver imported to Great Britain or Ireland had to be assayed and marked in a British assay office.
- From 1904 until 1973 all imported silver had to be marked with its relevant standard in decimal: .958 for Britannia silver and .925 for sterling silver. This system has recently undergone a review.

AESTHETIC STYLE
- **Period** Popular style in both Europe and the USA from *c*.1875 to the late 1880s
- **Inspiration** Japanese art – elegant forms, stark unadorned designs
- **Decoration** usually only minimal

► RUSTIC DESIGNS
Produced in the rustic Arts and Crafts style of the late 19thC, this late Victorian tea-kettle on a mobile stand has been lightly constructed from silver plate in a shape that is reminiscent of earlier copper kettles. This utility tea-kettle can also be used on a hotplate, as it has a flat base. $160–320

◄ JAPANESE STYLE
In the late 19thC, following the introduction of Japanese art to the West, firms such as the Gorham Manufacturing Co., Tiffany & Co., and Dominick & Haff employed Japanese metalworkers to create such Oriental-style silver vessels as this stylish tea-kettle, using innovative decorative techniques. This example (originally part of a tea service made *c*.1880 by Gorham) is handmade with a simulated bamboo handle and spout and decorative mixed-metal ornamentation of copper, nickel, and patinated silver. It features a swing stand for tipping the pot forward. $4,800–6,400

► GEORG JENSEN
The unusual style and exceptional quality of this tea-kettle (1925–32) by the Danish maker Georg Jensen (1866–1935) make it highly desirable. The feet of the cage-like stand incorporating a burner are mounted in carved hardwood and have silver pads underneath to prevent the table from being scorched. Pieces made by well-known designers who worked for Jensen, such as C.F. Hallberg or H. Nielsen, add a premium to vessels such as this one, and their stamped initials are frequently incorporated with the Jensen marks. Check also for English import marks, which will make it possible to date the piece exactly. Jensen's early production from the 1920s is rare and more keenly sought by collectors than that from the 1960s and 1970s, which is frequently copied from earlier designs. $4,800–6,400

TEA-URNS

Tea-urns, which were first introduced in the mid-18thC, were not for brewing tea but for providing a supply of hot water to replenish teapots and coffeepots. Generally larger and much less portable than tea-kettles, they have a horizontal tap (spigot) near the base for drawing hot water more safely than tilting a full kettle. The earliest tea-urns were heated with charcoal burners, but from the 1770s a heated iron rod (billet) was inserted into a socket or tube inside the urn, around which hot water circulated. Most urns are vase-shaped on a stemmed foot, with restrained decoration of Classical ornament or an engraved coat-of-arms. Occasionally the spout of the tap is cast and chased in the form of an animal or a bird. Tea-urns sometimes formed an integral part of a 19thC tea service.

▶ VASE SHAPES

Vase-shaped tea-urns were introduced in the early 1770s. This small George III example, made c.1778, is based on the design of a two-handled cup with a domed cover topped by an acorn finial and an ivory-handled spout that was originally stained green. The beaded borders and reeded handles are typical Neo-classical decoration. The vase-shaped urn was very popular in North America in the Revolutionary period. $3,200–4,800

▼ BARREL URNS

Globular or barrel-shaped urns, such as this London silver example (1823), were made from the first half of the 19thC. The urn rests on a square pedestal raised on four supports and has lion mask handles. Also made in Sheffield plate and electroplate, they were popular until c.1840. $4,000–4,800

◀ ARTS AND CRAFTS

This original and desirable silver-and-ivory tea-urn, which was made in 1912 by Omar Ramsden, a leading silver designer and disciple of the British Arts and Crafts Movement, and Alwyn Carr, draws inspiration from the past in form and decoration. The vase-shaped Classical urn rests on a six-legged stand with burner, a reminder of the fashion for tea-kettles in the 18thC, and is decorated with an eclectic mix of Classical and medieval ornament. $8,800–10,400

COLLECTING

Tea-urns are generally not popular with collectors and can be fairly affordable, although unusual or imaginative examples still command high prices.

CONSTRUCTION

Tea-urns are characterized by a horizontal spigot (tap) near to the base of the body, which *was used to release water. They are typically larger than tea-kettles – this late Victorian Neo-classical-style* *example is particularly large – and were sometimes made in the 19thC as part of a tea service. $3,200–4,000*

Be sure to check that the internal fittings are intact.

This example is decorated around the shoulder with a band of embossed work.

The spigot, finial, and handles are often made of ivory or stained hardwood such as apple or pear, which serves to insulate the user from the very hot metal.

The water for tea would be heated by lifting off the cover and placing the billet into the cylindrical socket. The finial stops the heat escaping.

Many tea-urns were produced in Sheffield plate because the cost of making such a large item in silver was frequently prohibitive.

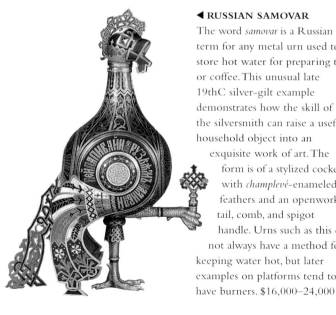

◀ **RUSSIAN SAMOVAR**
The word *samovar* is a Russian term for any metal urn used to store hot water for preparing tea or coffee. This unusual late 19thC silver-gilt example demonstrates how the skill of the silversmith can raise a useful household object into an exquisite work of art. The form is of a stylized cockerel with *champlevé*-enameled feathers and an openwork tail, comb, and spigot handle. Urns such as this do not always have a method for keeping water hot, but later examples on platforms tend to have burners. $16,000–24,000

CONVERSIONS

● Watch out for tea-urns that have been converted from two-handled cups by attaching spigots and lids.
● Some tea-urns have been changed into cups by the insertion of a plate of silver or "patch" over the hole left by the spigot. Such patches are often disguised with engraving.
● In some cases tea-urns have been fitted with electrical elements, and these conversions are best left well alone.

TEA-CADDIES, CADDY & MOTE SPOONS

Caddies were used for storing tea, which was imported in large chests and sold loose. Most early caddies were small, reflecting the high cost of tea. From the 1730s they were made in sets with a canister for blending tea or holding sugar, and stored in lockable wooden boxes decorated with exotic veneers. Early caddies were bottle shaped, but from the 1730s box, bombé or vase shapes chased with Rococo or chinoiserie decoration were more typical. From the 1770s caddies were no longer fitted into boxes but were made lockable. Neo-classical drum and oval forms were in vogue in the 1770s and 1780s, and in the Victorian period novelties were popular. Caddy spoons, small enough to fit inside caddies, were made from c.1770, when caddies no longer had caps for measuring and dispensing tea.

◀ EARLY TEA-CADDIES

Tea-caddies resembling Chinese porcelain tea-bottles such as this early example (1708) by the London maker William Fawdry had sliding bases or tops for filling the caddy and pull-off rounded caps that were used to measure the tea. Initially made in pairs and sets of three (highly prized), caddies were sometimes marked with the initials "G" and "B" to distinguish between the two types of tea available to European drinkers: unfermented green tea or the less-expensive, fermented black variety. Many caddies were fitted with lead liners to keep the tea fresh, but few of these survive. The price of this caddy reflects its quality and rarity. $2,400–3,200

RARE AMERICAN TEA-CADDY BY S. KIRK & SON

This fine Rococo-style tea-caddy of flaring cylindrical form with acanthus-clad bird's-head handles is by the Baltimore firm of S. Kirk & Son, one of the oldest and most celebrated American companies. This caddy is not in what is known as the "Kirk Style", characterized by profuse all-over embossing and chasing. It is marked with Kirk's mark, and as the firm used a variety of marks this helps with dating; those featured on this piece were used between 1846 and 1890. At 7¾in (20cm) in height and 42oz (1kg) in weight, this tea-caddy is extremely large and heavy, and consequently particularly desirable. $3,200–4,800

The interior features separate compartments with half-moon covers and ring handles.

Check such rare examples as this for restoration; have the feet been re-attached or the hinge repaired?

On the best examples the cover should fit the base snugly; beware of those that are too small or loose.

Notably, this tea-caddy is marked S. Kirk & Son on both the body and the base.

▶ **MASS-PRODUCED TEA-CADDIES**
This caddy, made in 1895 and decorated with die-stamped Classical ornament, is in a popular late 19thC form, but the quality of these mass-made pieces at this time was often inconsistent. Although mechanization made it possible to produce decorative silver more efficiently and cheaply than before, these designs were often flimsy and prone to damage. By the late 19thC most caddies were made without locks, as tea was less expensive than in the 18thC. $400–480

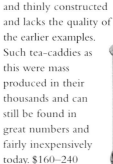

TEA MOTIFS
Tea-related ornament became popular in the late 18thC. Look out for caddies in the form of tea chests, and spoons decorated with tea-leaf shapes or plantation scenes.

▲ **CADDY SPOONS**
Although Birmingham was the main centre of British caddy-spoon production, this acorn–shaped example was made in London in 1807 by Elizabeth Morley. Most were stamped or raised from a thin sheet of silver and are fragile. Check for splits in the bowl or damaged handles, as repairs will drastically lower the value. $640–800

▶ **EDWARDIAN TEA-CADDIES**
Based on the form of a Chinese tea-bottle, this Edwardian caddy (1909) by the Chester firm of Nathan & Hayes recalls tea-caddies made in the 1720s. However, this example is very light and thinly constructed and lacks the quality of the earlier examples. Such tea-caddies as this were mass produced in their thousands and can still be found in great numbers and fairly inexpensively today. $160–240

◀ **MOTE SPOONS**
Mote spoons were used to skim floating tea leaves and tea dust (motes) off the surface of a cup of tea. They were a late 17thC invention and used mostly as part of tea-services. These examples feature typical mid-18thC decoration of pierced scrolls. "Picture" or "fancy back" mote spoons, with stamped designs on the back of the bowl, are much more desirable. Mote spoons are often found in fitted cases with tea-caddies and teaspoons. $320–400

BEWARE
Attempts are sometimes made to convert teaspoons into more valuable mote spoons. These conversions are usually easy to detect, but it is always best to seek expert advice when purchasing these collectible objects, especially if you have any doubts over the authenticity.

CHOCOLATE-POTS & COFFEEPOTS

Chocolate- and coffeepots are recorded from the 1650s, but few made before 1700 survive. Chocolate-pots, which mirror the styles and forms of coffeepots, are distinguished from coffeepots by hinged finials, which allowed a swizzle-stick or molinet to be inserted to stir the chocolate. Hinged finials were easily mislaid, and some were attached to the pots with silver chains. Chocolate-pots were rarely made in Britain after 1750, when the drink was no longer fashionable, and many were subsequently converted into coffeepots. The earliest coffeepots resembled Turkish wine jugs (with lips rather than spouts), but the teapot form, with a cover and a handle opposite the spout, soon became more popular. From its introduction in the 17thC coffee was flavored with sugar and spices and drunk with milk. From *c.*1800 most coffeepots were made as parts of matching tea services. As coffeepots were produced in large quantities, a great variety is available to the collector.

CHOCOLATE-POTS

Chocolate-pots are less frequently found in Britain than in continental Europe, where the drink was a more popular substitute for tea or coffee. The tapering cylindrical form of this George II piece is characteristic of chocolate-pots (and coffeepots) made before the 1730s. These pots were made of heavy-gauge silver, with a seam down the handle side of the pot; they featured cast-and-applied foot rims, straight or curving spouts, and hinged dome covers with finials. As a rule, earlier pots such as this one are more highly prized by collectors than the later pieces of the 1740s, as they are extremely rare. Some chocolate-pots were produced in sets with matching stands and burners, and all parts of the set should bear the same marks. $6,400–8,000

Most early chocolate-pots have domed lids. By the 1730s flat lids were more typical, with domed lids becoming popular again by *c.*1800.

Decoration is usually limited to engraved armorials or, occasionally, cut-card work around the handle. Check that the coat-of-arms is contemporary with the pot.

A cast-and-applied foot rim is typical of chocolate-pots made prior to the 1730s.

Hinged or pull-off finials facilitated the insertion of a swizzle-stick, so that the chocolate could be stirred before being poured. Marks on removable finials are desirable, especially on those made in the Britannia period (1697–1720).

Most handles are of fruitwood or ivory. Composition handles will be later replacements, but these do not necessarily lower the value of the pot.

◀ MOLINETS

To prevent chocolate from separating, it was mixed in the pot using a stirring-stick or molinet before being poured into cups. Molinets were inserted into the holes in the covers of pots, which were usually concealed by flaps or decorative hinged finials. This exquisite molinet with delicate pierced foliage was made in 1700 by Anthony Nelme of London. It is a great rarity and worth a handsome premium. $8,000–9,600

▶ BALUSTER SHAPES

The baluster shape with a tucked-in base and taller domed cover was a favoured form for coffeepots from the 1740s. The surface was usually decorated with gadrooned rims and flat-chased bands of Rococo ornamentation around the top and bottom of the body. This fine George II coffeepot was made in London in 1750 by Aymé Videau. Beware of later embossed work on plain 18thC pots. $3,200–4,800

▼ CAFE-AU-LAIT POTS

This charming Edwardian café-au-lait pot (one of a pair) is modeled on an 18thC baluster-shaped French chocolate- or coffeepot, with three feet, a small lip and a side handle. One pot was for coffee and the other for hot milk, and the two liquids would be poured in equal amounts at the same time. With its pair, this pot, which is decorated with embossed foliage and swirling scale-like strapwork, is highly desirable. $960–1,280

◀ THE PEAR SHAPE

The pear shape with a drop bottom, as exemplified by this elegant George III example of 1765 by the London makers William & James Priest, was a popular form for coffeepots from the 1760s. The gadrooned borders on the foot are also characteristic of coffeepots of this period. The slightly more elegant shape of this pot, compared with pots of an earlier date, signals the arrival of Neo-classicism. $1,800–4,200

COLLECTING

Look for chocolate-pots and coffeepots that combine elegant lines with quality. The weight, color, and original decoration will determine value, as will the name of an accomplished and reputable maker. Examine handle sockets and hinges for signs of wear, and check to see if a coat-of-arms has been erased, which leaves the silver thin and reduces the value considerably. Always check for a mark – for example, a lion passant or a maker's mark – on the cover.

CREAM JUGS & MILK JUGS

Cream and milk jugs were made from the early 18thC as a result of the increasing popularity of tea. The earliest form of cream jug was plain and pear-shaped or ovoid with a low foot rim and an applied handle and lip. Some jugs had hinged lids and wooden handles for serving hot milk, which before *c.*1720 was often taken with tea. Pear-shaped jugs were still common until the 1770s, but later 18thC examples had three cast feet, in the form of shells, scrolls, or pads, rather than low foot rims. Other mid-18thC vessels for holding cream include cow-creamers and cream-boats – the latter being a smaller version of a sauceboat, which was sometimes lavishly decorated with cast-and-chased Rococo shells, scrolls, and foliage. With the onset of Neo-classicism, cream jugs were made both in the shape of tapering urns and in vase form, with high loop handles and pedestal feet, sometimes on square plinths. From the 1790s most cream jugs were made as parts of matching tea services. Made of thin-gauge silver and subjected to heavy use, many jugs and creamers have been damaged, despite the beaded or reeded wires often applied to strengthen the rims.

◀ COW-CREAMERS

Cow-creamers were the speciality of John Schuppe (active 1753–73), a silversmith of Dutch origin working in London. Rare and collectible, these charming vessels have hinged covers on the backs of the cows, allowing them to be filled with cream; the curled-back tail acts as a handle, and the cow's mouth as a spout. The surfaces of these naively modeled jugs are found either plain or tooled to resemble the texture of animal hair; a few are found in silver gilt. $6,400–9,600

▶ CREAM PAILS

The bucket-shaped cream pail with a swing handle was popular from the mid-18thC. It was used mainly for clotted cream, which tended to keep fresh longer than ordinary cream at a time when there was no refrigeration. In the 1770s cream pails such as this one were often pierced with trelliswork and embossed with Chinese pastoral scenes or views of the English countryside. This pail would originally have had a blue-glass liner and possibly also a matching spoon or cream ladle. $1,600–2,400

LOOK OUT FOR

Piggins, which were used to hold clotted cream, are a variation on the cream pail. Fairly small in size, they were made in the form of a washtub. They were popular from the 1740s until the 1760s, particularly in Scotland, and are quite rare today. Scottish examples are particularly sought after.

▶ LAVISH DESIGNS

This silver-gilt George II cream jug is extravagantly decorated with a feast of cast-and-chased rocaille ornament and a scroll handle made of a cherub mask and an entwined lizard. The superb quality of this vessel, which resembles a ewer made in 1735 by the celebrated silversmith George Wickes, would certainly fetch a premium. Such jugs were made in a vast range of decorative styles, often en suite with a teapot or coffeepot. $6,400–8,000

BEWARE

Forgeries and conversions of pitcher-style cream jugs are occasionally found. These have usually been made by adding a lip to a christening mug, or a lip and handle to the body of a sugar, salt, or pepper caster. Be sure to check for splitting in the rim, and repairs around the handle joints. Also look to see that the foot has not been pushed into the body of the jug.

▶ MILK JUGS

The helmet shape, angular handle, reeded rim and fluting on the lower body of this late-Victorian milk jug copies a design that was very popular from *c*.1800 to 1815. The practical nature of the design is underscored by the sturdy flat base, which would easily sit on a tray without tipping over and spilling the milk. $160–210

▲ PROPORTIONS

Although this beautifully fashioned cream jug by Charles Boyton (1938) echoes early 18thC designs in the helmet shape, size, and proportions, its capacity would be much greater than that of earlier jugs. The body and foot have been raised from flat discs of silver, with the handle and decorative leafy bands cast separately. $960–1,280

◀ CHARACTER JUGS

Character jugs were made in considerable numbers in the late 19thC, particularly in Germany and The Netherlands. Typically imitating pottery versions, they were widely popular, although many were impractical and poorly made. This amusing head resembles contemporary images of Mr Punch and would no doubt have added great merriment to the tea-time ceremony. $480–640

SUGAR BOWLS & BASKETS

Sugar was stored in a box until the late 17thC, when the fashion for drinking tea led to the introduction of the sugar bowl – until that time the consumption of sugar was largely associated with sweet drinks such as punch. The earliest sugar bowls were hemispherical, resembling a porcelain tea bowl, and were usually simply decorated with only engraved coats-of-arms. Most had loose reversible covers; these were surmounted by rings, which could be used for holding teaspoons; however, few bowls with covers survive today.

The urn-shaped sugar bowl topped with a finial instead of a ring became popular in the mid-18thC, but by the 1770s this type of sugar holder had been replaced by a boat-shaped basket with a short stem and a swing handle. Sugar baskets, which are fashioned from plain sheet silver, are often decorated with pierced festoons and stylized leaves and flowers, and are fitted with glass liners; they remained popular throughout the 19thC, although at this period containers for sugar were usually produced as parts of tea or coffee services.

◀ SUGAR BOWLS

The elegant form of this George II sugar bowl, with plain shaped sides, low domed cover, and raised foot, has evolved from the early 18thC conservative bowls engraved with coats-of-arms. Lavishly decorated with the characteristic ornament of the Rococo – flower garlands, shells, scrolls, and a bud finial – this bowl was made in 1747 by Samuel Taylor of London and belongs to a tea-caddy set. In a cased set it would command a premium, although it is still fairly valuable on its own. $1,600–2,400

COLLECTING

● Sometimes original inscriptions are polished off to make way for new engraving. The silver then becomes thin and prone to creases and dents.
● Sugar bowls were often made as part of cased tea-caddy sets, consisting of a pair of tea caddies and a box or bowl either for sugar or for blending tea.

SCOTTISH & IRISH SUGAR BOWLS

A distinctive variation on the hemispherical sugar bowl form with an inverted lip is found in Scotland and Ireland but rarely in England. Most Irish examples are chased and stand on three feet, while in Scotland these sugar bowls usually feature a circular foot and are rarely decorated.

▶ SUGAR VASES

Sugar vases on pedestal bases became popular in the Neo-classical period. Decoration was minimal, confined to simple fluting or embossing and a decorative bud finial on the fitted cover. The upturned handles served as hooks or holders for sugar-sifter spoons (see pp. 108–9). Sugar vases such as this example of 1762 typically came in a suite of three, and a cased set of three would be very rare and desirable. $9,600–12,800

▼ SUGAR BASKETS
Boat-shaped sugar baskets, which had swing handles and were either plain or with simple engraved decoration, came into fashion in the late 18thC. This partially gilded example made in 1873 is identical in form to baskets produced in the 1780s, but the wavy rim, bat's-wing fluting, and mix of decorative motifs speak more to Victorian taste. Many sugar baskets produced during the Victorian period were pierced with decorative foliage and flowers and fitted with glass liners; they were often used for holding sweetmeats as well as sugar. Sugar baskets paved the way for the development of the open sugar bowl in the 19thC. $400–560

▶ NOVELTY DESIGNS
This double-ended electroplated sugar scuttle (*c.*1875) with mounted wooden handle and scoop is by the renowned designer Christopher Dresser. It is a quirky variation on the basket style, featured above, for which the Victorians were renowned. $960–1,280

CHARLES, THOMAS, AND GEORGE FOX
The mark below, which features the initials "GF" for "George Fox" (*d.*1910), is one of the marks of the London-based Fox family firm (est. *c.*1801). The firm is especially reputed for its quality decorative wares made during the Victorian era.

GF

◀ COCONUT BOWLS
This variation on the popular open sugar bowl was made by George Fox in the 1860s, and illustrates the Victorian taste for the exotic. Made from a coconut shell, the sugar bowl has been lavishly mounted with garlands of silver roses, acanthus leaves, a beaded rim, and reeded handles. It was probably part of a set, which would have included a matching cream jug and teapot or coffeepot. $320–480

SUGAR CASTERS & TOOLS

A variety of devices have been employed for serving sugar. Sugar casters, so-called because they "cast" their contents over the food, first appeared in sets of three, with two smaller casters for pepper and mustard, in the second half of the 17thC. The popularity of the caster waned towards the end of the 18thC. Most sugar casters feature engraved coats-of-arms. Single casters are desirable, but complete sets are even more highly prized. Other items for serving sugar include sugar nips and sugar tongs, both of which were employed to lift a lump of sugar from a sugar bowl. Early tongs were made from the late 17thC; nips were produced from the early 18thC. Another ingenious device was the sugar-sifter spoon, which was used to sprinkle powdered sugar over sour fruit. Sugar-sifter spoons are often found in fitted cases alongside spoons for serving fruit.

LIGHTHOUSE SUGAR CASTER

Sometimes called a sugar sifter or dredger, the lighthouse-shaped sugar caster became a popular form from the late 17thC. The plain body of this American example, made

c.1700 by the New York silversmith Jacobus Van der Spiegel who was of Dutch origin, offered a generous surface for engraving a coat-of-arms – an essential decorative feature of dining plate. Very little American silver made

before the War of Independence (1775–83) survives, and this is the largest of only four American sugar casters that are known to exist from the first quarter of the 18thC; it is therefore exceptionally valuable. $128,000–192,000

For maximum value the finial should be in good condition and unrestored.

Lighthouse sugar casters are sometimes also known as cylindrical casters, after their shape.

Good engraving of a coat-of-arms adds to the value, especially if it is a traceable crest, as here – this coat-of-arms is probably that of the Gardiner family of Gardiner's Island, New York. Make sure that the coat-of-arms is contemporary with the piece. Silver that has been re-engraved will be thin; this you can feel by pressing the surface.

Check that the inside cover has not been repaired and that the piercing is undamaged.

The top of this sugar caster is attached to the base by means of a bayonet joint, whereby two vertical lugs on the cover fit into slots on the base and are then twisted to ensure that they stay in place. Check that the cover fits the base snugly.

ARTS AND CRAFTS AND LIBERTY & CO.

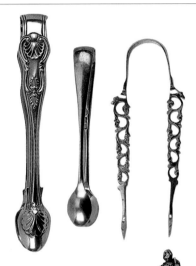

In reaction against the poor-quality metalware mass-manufactured during the Victorian period, exponents of the Arts and Crafts style aimed to revive the use of high-quality materials, good craftsmanship and a return to traditional handicraft techniques. By 1904 one of the leading pioneers of the style was the firm of Liberty & Co., founded in 1875 in London's Regent Street by Arthur Lasenby Liberty and still in operation there today. Such items as this vase-shaped sugar caster were commissioned by the firm from well-known artists and are extremely sought after among collectors.

Although this example has the same pear shape and sloping slanted cover found on examples from the Queen Anne period of the late 17th and early 18thC, the decorative cabochon turquoise finial, which is characteristically Arts and Crafts, betrays its later date. $1,920–3,200

▶ SUGAR TONGS

Sugar tongs, which are widely available, are easily damaged, and if repaired are worth little, making them among the most affordable silver available to collectors. Scottish and Irish provincial tongs are more expensive and highly sought after. On the pierced example far right (1765) the arms have been cast separately and soldered onto a U-shaped spring section. Cast-arm tongs such as these are very sought after in good condition but tend to have flaws or damage. $80–110 (each)

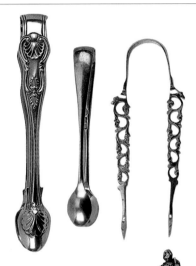

◀ SUGAR NIPS

Early sugar nips have straight arms, are very delicate and are rare and valuable, especially if they bear a maker's mark. This pair from the 1750s adopts an early style, but is decorated with scrolls typical of the Rococo period. Victorian sugar nips were made in many elaborate forms. Nips made in the USA are particularly sought after. $160–240

▶ SUGAR-SIFTER SPOON

This sugar-sifter spoon (1863) is by Francis Higgins. Beware of converted sauce ladles, which have been pierced at a later date with a scrolling pattern. These are easy to spot, as the bowl of a sugar-sifter spoon is generally flatter and shallower than that of a sauce ladle. $160–240

From the middle of the 18thC wine became increasingly popular in Britain, and consequently silver vessels and gadgets associated with wine drinking were produced in vast quantities. The service of wine was an elaborate and ceremonious procedure demanding its own individual silver items in many forms, from massive coolers to jugs and ewers for serving wine and spirits, wine coasters for holding glass decanters, funnels for decanting the wine, tiny silver bottle tickets and collars for labeling, and corkscrews for opening bottles. A variety of wines was often served to complement the different dishes of each dinner course, thus increasing the need for a range of designs from which to serve each beverage, and on the sideboards of the grandest houses the largest and most impressive objects were often associated with serving wine. Wine coolers developed from the monumental and impressive wine cisterns of the late 17thC, which were used for washing glasses or cooling several bottles of wine in iced water. Originally a French refinement, wine coolers were largely produced by immigrant Huguenot silversmiths in the early 18thC. Other vessels used for cooling or serving wine include jugs, ewers, monteiths, and punchbowls. Decoration of Bacchanalian motifs (vine leaves and bunches of grapes, for example) is particularly characteristic. Many of these silver items associated with the wine trade were produced in large numbers and are still readily available today, making this a highly popular area of collecting.

WINE COOLERS

Most wine coolers are based on the form of an antique calyx crater or bucket shape, although a popular version was made in imitation of the Warwick vase. All wine coolers were made with removable drop-in liners around which ice could be packed to chill the bottles. Early examples were made with separate collars, but by the early Victorian period the collars and liners were integrated into one. Many wine coolers were given as prizes or presentation pieces, with inscriptions that may enhance their value; most were made in pairs, and in general a single is much less desirable than a pair.

▲ **BUCKET-SHAPED WINE COOLERS**
Wine coolers in the form of a wooden bucket or pail were made in large quantities in old Sheffield plate, particularly in the last decade of the 18thC. Many are decorated with a swing handle and engraved vertical lines simulating the staves on a wooden pail or, as seen above, with reeded hoops and an engraved armorial. Liners were commonly made by folding a flat piece of plate into a cylinder – the vertical seam can just be detected on the interior of this example (c.1800). To economize on silver, the detachable liner and the inside of the cooler have been flashed with a layer of tin, producing the dark gray color. It is important to check that the collar and liner have not been replaced and, with silver examples, that they bear the same hallmarks as those found on the body of the cooler. $480–800

▶ CLASSICAL STYLE

Many coolers in the form of Greek vases or calyx craters were made in the Regency period (c.1790–1820). This fine George IV example, made in 1822 by the top London silversmith Benjamin Smith, is boldly chased with a scheme of Classical ornament – anthemion borders around the body, cast-and-applied beaded rims, and egg-and-dart patterns edging the foot and collar – and an engraved crest and motto. Classical ornamentation also features on the massive silver-gilt Regency coolers by makers such as Rundell, Bridge & Rundell and Paul Storr; most Victorian coolers combine Gothic or Egyptian styles with naturalistic decoration. $9,600–12,880

◀ QUALITY

This wine cooler – one of a pair made in 1820 by S.C. Younge & Co. – is lighter and not as robust as the one above. Sheffield makers used far less silver to produce wine coolers than other British silversmiths, as the handles and borders of acanthus leaves and flowers on their wares were die-stamped from a thin foil of silver, lead filled, and soldered, rather than cast or embossed. With regular use some Sheffield-made examples with elaborate decoration are prone to damage, so check for dents in the body, broken and repaired handles or cracked ornamentation. With its pair this wine cooler would weigh only slightly more than the single example in solid silver above, and be much less valuable. $1,920–2,400

OLD SHEFFIELD PLATE

By the 1820s Sheffield silversmiths were posing a serious threat to London makers by mass producing competing wares more cost-effectively. Sheffield-made silver, which used the same dies and stampings as the plating industry, was produced on a large scale without sacrificing quality to mechanization, and many wares such as this cooler (one of a pair made in the 1840s) were of very fine quality. Sheffield plate is now often referred to as old Sheffield plate to avoid confusion with electroplate on copper – patented c.1840 and sometimes now termed "Sheffield" or Sheffield plate by some 20thC manufacturers - which involves depositing a thin layer of silver by electrolysis onto metal or any other conductible medium. Notable makers of old Sheffield plate include the firms of J. Wright & G. Fairbairn and Messrs Creswick. $3,200–4,800

WRIGHT & FAIRBAIRN

CRESWICKS

WINE JUGS & EWERS

Large jugs intended to hold wine or beer came into use with the Restoration of the Monarchy in 1660. Some early examples have covers, but lidded jugs made after the 1730s are very rare. These jugs do not have insulated handles and were probably never designed to hold hot liquids; if a jug has an ivory handle it will be a later addition. Most 18thC jugs are baluster-shaped and until the reign of George II (1727–60) had plain bodies. The Rococo led to the production of more elaborate designs. Silver wine jugs with vine motifs came into fashion *c*.1830. Early examples are made of solid silver; later versions are glass with silver mounts. Ewers are large jugs with tall, deep lipped bowls, stemmed bases, handles, and, sometimes, lids.

▶ RARITIES

This extremely rare squat George I covered jug (1714), made by Simon Pantin in London, is simply engraved with an armorial within a cartouche surrounded by foliage and strapwork. In general a coat-of-arms or crest, as seen on this example, will not lower the value if contemporary with the piece; however, if such decoration has been polished out and re-engraved, the body may be very thin and prone to damage. The harp-shaped handles were popular until the 1750s, when the S-scroll form became more fashionable. Many such jugs were commissioned by the nobility from top-quality Huguenot makers. Collectors should watch out for early 18thC tankards that have had spouts added, or plain pear-shaped jugs that have lost their covers and had the hinges removed. $24,000–32,000

◀ NEO-CLASSICISM

During the Victorian period Neo-classicism enjoyed a popular revival, and many silver wares were produced in this style. This vase-shaped claret or wine jug, made in 1886, is decorated with engraved-and-chased Classical ornament of acanthus foliage, beaded borders, and swags, and has an insulated wooden handle so that it could also be used to hold hot liquids. It is less valuable than its early 18thC counterpart above, which has a solid silver handle and was intended only for cold liquids. $800–1,120

▶ LAVISH DESIGNS

After the Great Exhibition of 1851 in London the new styles based on the gargantuan display pieces were imitated by many silversmiths, sometimes in silver gilt. This ornate ewer (1855) is decorated after a Renaissance design with Classical figures, reliefs illustrating the triumphs of Neptune and Galatea, and a riot of ruffled scrolls, garlands and engraved armorials. Such lavish pieces were generally intended for show, given as presentation pieces or awarded as trophies. $4,800–8,000

◀ NOVELTY FORMS
Made in 1869 by Richard Sibley, this charming claret or wine jug, which is modeled as a griffin or wyvern, is superbly wrought with a hinged head, finely-textured plumage, and cast handle and feet. A coronet and monogram have been engraved on the tail. From the 1820s until the beginning of the 20thC silversmiths

adopted a variety of highly innovative ornamental styles, which afforded them ample opportunity to demonstrate their special skills. Classical, medieval and naturalistic forms were all great Victorian favorites, and a jug such as this one, which was produced by an accomplished silversmith, would command a high premium. $3,200–4,800

▶ CELLINI PATTERN
The Renaissance-inspired "Cellini" pattern was the most popular design for ewers and wine jugs throughout the 19thC. This silver-gilt example (1866) is richly cast with characteristic Renaissance ornament of masks, foliage, strapwork, beasts, and fruit, and a caryatid handle with a hinged cover. In some cases the earlier-style decoration on these

ewers was not always rendered accurately. This small ewer has been cast and is of excellent quality; other examples that have been stamped are lighter and not as eagerly sought after by collectors. This ewer would originally have been made with a set of matching wine goblets, and the full set would fetch a high price; it is nevertheless very desirable on its own. $3,200–4,000

MARKS
Birmingham designer Christopher Dresser (1834–1904) stressed function, economy of materials, and minimal decoration, which served mainly to strengthen a piece. His designs are usually stamped with his name or monogram, and they often also include a registration mark.

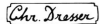

◀ DRESSER EWER
The simple, functional form of this glass ewer with silver mounts, made c.1880 by Christopher Dresser, makes it a popular alternative to the all-silver versions. Such ewers were popular from the 1850s until c.1900, and were often made in pairs in fitted boxes and given as presentation pieces or wedding presents. Numerous makers imitated this style, but ewers by Dresser are prized among collectors. $800–1,600

WINE TASTERS

Wine tasters have been employed by vintners for judging the taste, clarity, and color of wine since the 15thC, and the earliest surviving English silver example dates from 1603. Silver was considered to be the most suitable material for these shallow circular vessels, although they were frequently gilded on the inside to protect the silver from corrosion by the wine. The majority of wine tasters have raised domed centers that enable the color of the wine to be seen more easily; most designs with flat centers were intended predominately for decoration. Since wine tasters are very lightly constructed, they are prone to damage – the fragile wire handles are susceptible to breaking, and the decoration may have been polished away. Wine tasters that are not in good condition are not popular among collectors.

▶ QUAICHES

Resembling a shallow porringer, this plain, two-handled drinking vessel, known as a "quaich" (or "quaigh"), is a form that originated in Scotland. Small quaiches were for individual use, while larger ones were passed round on ceremonial occasions. The very earliest examples were made of wood and featured vertical staves, silver rims, and silver-mounted handles. This quaich, which was manufactured by the firm of Hamilton & Inches of Edinburgh in 1894, is a popular design that was frequently given as a christening present. Scottish provincial silver is keenly sought by collectors, and examples made in the late 17th or early 18thC are rare and command very high prices. $320–400

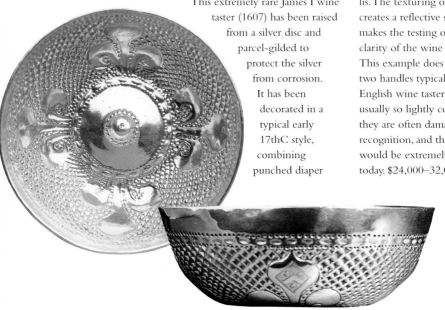

▼ RARE SURVIVORS

This extremely rare James I wine taster (1607) has been raised from a silver disc and parcel-gilded to protect the silver from corrosion. It has been decorated in a typical early 17thC style, combining punched diaper ornament with chased fleurs-de-lis. The texturing on the bowl creates a reflective surface that makes the testing of the color and clarity of the wine more accurate. This example does not feature the two handles typical of most English wine tasters. They are usually so lightly constructed that they are often damaged beyond recognition, and this rare survivor would be extremely valuable today. $24,000–32,000

ENGLISH/FRENCH
The following points can help with identification:
English
- usually two handles
- body decoration of chased fluting or a pattern of circular bosses on one side

French
- mid- to end 18thC: shaped handle with a flange at the top (the value increases if the flange is engraved with a motto, message, initials, a name, or pastoral scenes); late 18th and 19thC: ring handle
- typically undecorated

▲ PUNCHED DECORATION
This Charles II wine taster was made in 1677 by William Maddox, who produced such items in great numbers; fully marked examples are highly desirable. The two S-shaped handles on this piece have been constructed from thin strips of wire, and the combination of punched decoration with a plain silver surface lends the wine taster a two-dimensional effect. The decoration around the body is characteristic of English designs. $3,200–4,800

▶ MINIATURE DESIGNS
A number of silversmiths, including David Clayton and George Manjoy, were renowned for making miniature versions of larger vessels, such as this small wine taster. The wire handles often break off, and the decoration has sometimes rubbed away, which is detrimental to the value. Fully marked tasters in good condition (as here) are very collectible. $2,400–3,200

◀ FRENCH WINE TASTERS
This typical French wine taster (1770) is undecorated and has a shaped handle with a flange on top for the thumb. At the end of the 18thC and throughout the 19thC French wine tasters commonly had a ring handle, in the form of a serpent, without the flange. Rare marked provincial examples are extremely valuable, as are those made prior to the French Revolution in 1789. Wine tasters such as this were intended to be hung on a ribbon around the neck. $1,280–1,920

WINE COASTERS

Wine coasters were decorative yet protective devices made for passing wine bottles or decanters around the table and ensuring that wine did not spill on the table or linen. They evolved from early bottle stands and were made in great numbers, in pairs or sets, from the mid-18thC. Most coasters have rounded wooden bases, which are sometimes inlaid with crested silver discs or bosses for engraving and have baize linings underneath to protect furniture from scratches, and silver galleried sides. Many coasters produced from the 1780s were embellished with Neo-classical ornament such as beaded or reeded borders, urn motifs, and leaf patterns. Some sumptuous silver-gilt wine coasters with heavy cast sides and engraved bases of silver were made in the Regency period (c.1790–1820). Wine coasters continue to be made in earlier styles and are a popular collecting area.

▶ POPULAR DESIGNS

The simple circular form of this pair of silver-and-wood wine coasters (1798), decorated with reeded bands and bright-cut engraved vine leaves, was a winning formula in the late 18th and early 19thC and is still a much-produced design today. If a coaster has a wooden base, check the condition of the wood, especially to see whether it has shrunk. Although the condition of the wood does not greatly affect the value – and worn or split wood can be easily replaced – it does give an indication of how much the coaster has been used. $1,920–2,400

WHY THE NAME "COASTER"?

Early coasters were known as "stands" or "slides". The term "coaster" dates only from 1887 and is derived from the custom that the ladies would retire from the table after dinner, the tablecloth would be removed, and a bottle of port "coasted" around the table by the men.

◀ WIREWORK

Silversmiths experimented with wirework from the 1790s, and these coasters from a set of four made in London in 1799 have wirework galleries held with a guard rings at the top instead of enclosed sides. The wooden discs with gadrooned borders are inset with silver bosses for an engraved initial or crest. $6,400–9,600

▶ GRAPE AND VINE-LEAF MOTIFS

One of the most popular motifs featured on silver associated with serving wine and spirits is that of grapes and vines. Images of the god of wine Bacchus (Dionysus) are also characteristic. This silver-plated wine coaster, which is one of a pair by the Birmingham firm of Elkington & Co. (est. c.1830), has been cast with an openwork pattern of grapes and vine leaves. Silver-gilt versions with gilded bases were popularized by the English firm of Rundell, Bridge & Rundell. $640–800 (for a pair)

▶ **WINE-GLASS COASTERS**
These American coasters – part
of a set of twelve by the Baltimore
firm of S. Kirk & Son – were
designed to hold drinking glasses
rather than wine bottles or
decanters and are smaller than
coasters for bottles. The glass
bases are cut with a star motif that
allows air to escape and thus stops
the coasters sticking to the wine-
glass when wet. $240–320
(for a set)

▲ **COASTER TROLLEYS**
The innovative design of this
silver-plated coaster trolley with
pierced basket-shaped carriages
to hold wine decanters was an
effective novelty for the dining
table that is highly sought after
today. This example was probably
made by Elkington & Co. in the
1850s, although large elaborate
versions were produced earlier
by such
well-known
silversmiths as Paul
Storr and Benjamin Smith.
Variations on this design include
double decanter coasters on
a single wooden base, and a
coaster trolley known as the
"jolly boat" in the shape of
a rowing boat on four small
wheels. $2,400–3,200

COLLECTING
● Wine coasters are
extremely saleable objects
and in demand among
collectors.
● All coasters were
manufactured either
in pairs or in sets, and a
pair or set will be much
more valuable than a
single coaster.

▶ **REVIVAL STYLES**
Wine coasters are still produced
in vast numbers today, in a host
of traditional styles, in both silver
and silver plate. This pair of
coasters made in 1931 has
the pierced gallery that was
favoured in the 1780s, although
plain versions with engraved
decoration and those with vine-
leaf motifs are also very popular.
$640–800

MONTEITHS & PUNCHBOWLS

Monteiths and punchbowls were first produced in Britain in the late 17thC, after punch (made from brandy, red wine, spices, sugar, and lemon or orange juice) was introduced from India. Punch became a popular drink and was often mixed by the host at the table after dinner. Monteiths, made from the 1680s, are large bowls with notched rims from which wine glasses could be hung by their stems and cooled in iced water; they supposedly take their name from a Scotsman called Monteigh, who was famed for wearing a cloak with a scalloped hem. Some examples were made with detachable crenelated collars, which allowed them to be used as punchbowls. Both the bowl of the monteith and the detachable rim should be fully hallmarked. Punchbowls have fixed, straight (as opposed to scalloped) rims and are usually deeper than monteiths. Many were made as presentation pieces, and some were made with matching ladles. Early punchbowls from the late 17thC are rare and tend to be decorated with embossed work; those made from the 18thC were usually not so elaborately decorated or shaped.

◀ EARLY MONTEITHS

Many early monteiths such as this Queen Anne (1702–14) example were decorated with fluted panels on the body for added strength, cast lion-mask handles, an applied beaded foot rim, and an engraved coat-of-arms. Check for an armorial that has been removed, which makes the silver quite thin. $24,000–40,000

▶ LATER MONTEITHS

Few monteiths were made after the 1730s, although they enjoyed a revival in France in the late 18th and early 19thC, and they were rarely produced in old Sheffield plate. Reproductions such as this example from the late Victorian period were made to emulate monteiths from the early 18thC. The crenelated collar, which in this case is not detachable, and the fluting on the body echo an earlier decorative style, although on this version the more realistic rendering of the lion-mask handles and the swirled fluting indicate a later date. In the late 19th and early 20thC, reproductions similar to this monteith became extremely popular as wedding presents. $2,400–3,200

◀ VERRIERES

The influence of Neo-classicism is evident in the oval boat-shaped form, loop handles and band of laurel ornament around the body of this late 18thC French monteith, known as a *verrière*. This example is one of a pair, which considerably increases its value. $4,800–6,400

◀ PUNCH LADLES

These George III punch ladles have stems fashioned from twisted whalebone. The bowls have been raised from silver coins, with another coin inset at the bottom where the silver has then been made very thin by hammering. The ladle on the right has also been decorated with embossed fluting and a beaded rim for extra strength. Ladles produced from coins were made in large numbers from the 1760s. As punch ladles are light and flimsy, most are damaged and are not especially valuable today. Fully marked better-quality examples from the early 18thC – many decorated with embossed scenes or bright-cut engraving – are more desirable and fetch a higher price. $160–800 (each)

▲ PUNCHBOWLS

The shape of this George I example, with only a coat-of-arms for decoration, is typical of an early 18thC punchbowl – over time the bowls became larger and the feet higher. Today punchbowls are often found gilded inside, but this was a later fashion with the purpose of protecting the interior from corrosion caused by the acidity of wine in the punch. Many later punchbowls were made as prizes or presentation pieces. Most 18thC punchbowls are marked underneath in the points of a compass. The earliest punchbowls, and many later examples, are marked in a straight line below the rim; however, these marks have sometimes been rubbed away by over-zealous cleaning. $16,000–24,000

COLLECTING

● Detachable collars on monteiths should be fully marked with the same hallmarks as the main body.
● Be suspicious of punchbowls that are totally without decoration – bowls usually feature at least an engraved coat-of-arms or armorial.

◀ TIFFANY & CO.

This extravagant punchbowl by Tiffany & Co., decorated with nautical imagery, was commissioned by a New York shipping firm. Like many 19thC punchbowls it was made c.1880 as a presentation prize, to commemorate an important win in a yachting tournament, and the all-over decorative scheme echoes this theme. What makes this example especially valuable is the extraordinary quality of hand craftsmanship that has gone into its production, and that is typical of Arts and Crafts wares. Such pieces in unusual designs, which are made at least partly by hand by such American firms as Tiffany or Gorham Manufacturing Co., are keenly sought after and fetch very high sums. $64,000–96,000

MISCELLANEOUS I

Silversmiths created many gadgets and tools to complement the often elaborate ceremony of drinking wine, punch, and spirits. These items included funnels for decanting wine from a bottle to be served at the table (keenly sought after by wine buffs), pierced lemon-and orange-juice strainers and nutmeg graters for the preparation of spiced wine and punches, and cradles for holding bottles or decanters. Other collectible items include kovsches for serving wine, and brandy saucepans, for both warming brandy and mulling wine. Check the condition of these items, as many of them will have been subjected to extensive use.

▶ WINE FUNNELS

Wine funnels were produced in great numbers from the late 18thC until *c.*1830. Made in two parts – a funnel and a pierced bowl to strain the sediment – they are minimally decorated with beaded or reeded rims on early examples, or perhaps some chased ornamentation around the bowls on later funnels. A typical funnel from the George III period could have a straight ogee bowl, as on this example made in 1819 by the London firm of Emes & Barnard, or a plain tulip- or dome-shaped bowl. The curved spout allows the wine to trickle down the side of the decanter, although as the necks of decanters became narrower, these spouts were sometimes trimmed. $800–1,600

◀ MINI WINE FUNNELS

This late Victorian wine funnel was manufactured in Birmingham and, although small, is practical. Its primary purpose was to facilitate the filling of hip flasks with spirits; it was also used to add perfume to scent bottles. A variation of this type is a tiny funnel made for traveling sets, especially in France, and used to fill perfume *nécessaires*. These funnels are not very collectible and can be purchased at quite a low price. $130–160

▼ STRAINERS

Most early strainers are perforated with a simple dot pattern and have only one handle, with a hook or ring on the opposite side that would be clipped onto the rim of the punchbowl; later ones such as this mid-18thC example have two handles. Few strainers were made after 1800, as by then drinking punch was no longer in vogue. $800–1,120

COLLECTING FUNNELS

• Provincial wine funnels, magnum funnels, and funnels made in the USA, Scotland, Ireland, or by known makers are most desirable.
• The bowl, spout, and collar (if appropriate) should all be marked.

▲ BOTTLE CRADLES
The bottle cradle, designed to hold an open bottle of wine during the meal, is both a useful and a decorative item for the dining table. A late Victorian invention, it was produced in numerous variations, including those with winding mechanisms, which proved to be very impractical. Most wine cradles, as this example, were made in silver plate and frequently embellished with flowers, fruits, and vines. $160–240

CLOISONNE ENAMELING
This ancient technique, used notably by Byzantine and Celtic craftsmen, is achieved as follows:
i) The design is outlined by soldering metal strips onto a metal base to create a network of compartments, known as "cells" or *cloisons*.
ii) The *cloisons* are filled in with colored enamels, but the tops of the metal strips are left exposed.
iii) The piece is fired and then polished smooth.

CONDITION
• Strainers should be fully hallmarked on the bowl, but sometimes marks have been lost in the pierced decoration. The handles are susceptible to damage.
• Look for alterations – a funnel with a trimmed spout will worth less than one in original condition.

▶ KOVSCHES
Of Russian origin and popular until the mid-18thC, kovsches are one-handled boat-shaped vessels used for ladling out wine and spirits. This *cloisonné*-enameled silver-gilt version was made *c.*1895 by Fedor Ruckert, who was well known for shaded enamel decoration. $1,600–1,920

◀ BRANDY SAUCEPANS
Brandy saucepans – also known as "pipkins" – are small saucepans used for warming brandy or mulling wine. Most have bowls that bulge at the bottom, with lips for pouring, wooden, or ivory handles and usually silver covers (rarely still with the saucepan). Many feature engraved decoration on the bowls. $1,280–1,920

MISCELLANEOUS II

Other wine collectibles include wine labels and corkscrews. The earliest wine labels (known as "bottle tickets") were handwritten on parchment, but these were replaced in the 1740s by silver labels, which were suspended around the necks of the bottles on chains, with the name of the wine or spirit engraved or pierced. Designs include the more common escutcheon, oval, and crescent shapes, as well as masks, shells, scrolls, anchors, and vine leaves; more than a thousand names have been recorded. Originally called "steele wormes" or bottle screws, corkscrews come in a variety of forms and designs, some with additional attachments for multiple use, such as a button hook or tobacco tamper.

▲ WINE-BOTTLE COLLARS

The earliest wine labels ("bottle tickets") were handwritten on parchment to identify wine. The employment of a silver label bearing the name of the drink in a bottle and hung on a chain around the bottle neck, began in the 1740s. A variation on the wine label on a chain, the wine-bottle collar or ring became popular during the Regency period (c.1790–1820). Many wine-bottle collars were gilded and lavishly decorated with scrolls, putti, and such drink-related motifs as grapes and vine leaves. A set of three or four labels is especially valuable. $1,280–1,600

▼ DECANTER LABELS

Bottle labels such as this one for rum were made to hang around the necks of bottles on chains. They were stamped out from sheets of silver in great numbers during the Victorian period, and were often made in sets of six or ten. Labels made to hang from the necks of decanters are slightly larger and even more lavishly decorated with scrolls or foliage. $45–65

◀ LIQUEUR LABELS

Wine labels featuring more obscure names such as "Rhenish", "Orange", and "Shrub" are more valuable than those bearing common titles such as sherry, port, or madeira. Labels for homemade wines or rare dessert wines often bear amusing titles and can be very collectible. Early labels are rare and demand high prices, as do provincial labels from Scotland or Ireland. Specialist makers such as Sandylands Drinkwater or Margaret Binley are keenly sought after, as are heavier cast Regency labels by Paul Storr or Benjamin Smith. $1,600–2,400

◀ SIZE AND DECORATION
Many corkscrews are pocket size, which makes them useful for traveling or picnics, although some larger ones intended for use in taverns or wine cellars were also made. Silver corkscrews are often decorated with engraved or chased decoration, and this George III example, which was made *c.*1790 by Joseph Taylor in Birmingham, is embellished with beading, fluting, and mother-of-pearl ornament. $480–640

▼ ART DECO CORKSCREWS
Made in the 1940s by R.E. Stone, this corkscrew has been designed in the angular, architectural Art Deco style. It was originally part of a set, which also included a matching bottle-cap lifter for removing metal caps. Corkscrews have an enthusiastic following among collectors, and can be found in many styles at a range of prices. $160–800

▲ NOVELTY CORKSCREWS
Many corkscrews were made in novelty form, such as this charming early 20thC design. The scales, fins, and tail of the salmon are delicately rendered, and the fish winks with eyes made of garnets. Corkscrews such as this one in fitted cases are much sought after, as they make excellent gifts. $480–640

BIRMINGHAM SILVER
The Birmingham assay office, established in 1773 largely due to the influence of the local manufacturer Matthew Boulton, reinforced the city's reputation as a center of silver production. By 1773 there were more than 2,000 silver firms in the city, specializing in small silverware including buckles, caddy spoons, vinaigrettes, and bottle labels. The town mark for Birmingham is an upright anchor. It is usually shown with the lion rampant, a date letter, duty mark (sovereign's head), and maker's mark.

Drinking Vessels

Drinking vessels have always been made in large numbers, essentially for everyday use. Over the centuries their basic design has changed little, and in general they do not feature the elaborate decoration seen on more prestigious dining plate. Among the earliest drinking vessels are beakers (drinking vessels without handles, stems, or foots), with only a few surviving from the 15thC. Tankards, which date from the mid–16thC, are distinguished by hinged covers and handles and are mostly plain, although some Victorian examples are elaborately decorated in revival styles. Goblets, also made from the mid–16thC, are characterized by bowls (usually semi-ovoid) on stemmed feet. Mugs, which are one-handled but lidless, date from the mid–17thC. Early mugs are bulbous and derive from contemporary pottery forms. Porringers, which take their name from *potager* (French for "soup bowl"), are two-handled vessels made in the late 17thC; in the USA they are often known as "caudle" cups. Cups are difficult to define, as presentation cups and drinking vessels made for special occasions are often given the name regardless of their forms. In theory a cup has two or more handles, but this is disproved by the most basic form – the tumbler cup – and by the elaborate cups designed for wagers. In the 18thC, when tea and coffee were more popularly drunk than beer, many mugs and tankards were given as christening presents. Today drinking vessels are popularly collected, although heavy use has left many damaged, which makes it vital to look for pieces without wear or damage such as split rims or cracked handles.

PORRINGERS & MUGS

Porringers are two-handled cylindrical cups produced between *c.*1650 and *c.*1750 to hold soup or caudle. The earliest British mugs date from the mid–17thC, and until *c.*1800 most were fairly plain. Most common in the early 18thC were baluster-shaped mugs with cast handles and only engraved coats-of-arms or initials for decoration. In the late 18thC mugs and their handles were made from cylinders of sheet metal, and in the 19thC small, often lavishly decorated examples were popularly given as christening presents.

▲ **RARE US CUPS**
Caudle was a mix of wine or ale, spices, and sugar, given from *c.*1650 to *c.*1700 to invalids and women convalescing after childbirth. It was served from a baluster-shaped, two-handled bowl, which often had a cover to keep the caudle warm. This example by the New York maker Gerrit Onckelbag (*c.*1700) is extremely rare – fewer than 12 American caudle cups are known. Decoration is restricted to the cast handles and an armorial. Americans often borrowed heraldic devices by looking up their name in *Guillim's Display of Heraldry.*
$10,400–20,000

MARKS
In the USA it was customary for makers to stamp their wares with their own marks. Silver by Gerrit Onckelbag is marked "BGO".

B
G O

▶ PORRINGERS
Porringers were often given as presents to women following the birth of a child. Like caudle cups, porringers are two-handled bowls, sometimes with covers, but they have straight sides and are larger and deeper. Used for a variety of drinks or thick soups, porringers were still made well into the 18thC. In the USA a shallow bowl with a pierced handle is known as a porringer, although it is called a bleeding bowl in Britain. The light body and thin handles of this 18thC porringer are fragile and susceptible to damage, which would be detrimental to the value. $1,280–1,920

◀ THISTLE MUGS
In the late 17th and early 18thC small vessels known as "thistle" mugs were made principally in Scotland. These mugs (such as this one of 1694) are of flaring form with a central applied band; the lower body is decorated with applied flutes imitating thistles. Thistle mugs are quite rare, with provincial Scottish examples most coveted. $3,200–8,000 (provincial thistle mugs may fetch over $16,000)

▶ CHRISTENING MUGS
From the 1830s until *c.*1900 it was *de rigueur* in Britain and the USA to give silver mugs as christening presents, sometimes in a cased set with a knife, fork and spoon. Mugs featuring mottos such as "Pause, ponder, sift!" are more commercial than those that are simply initialled. This mug of baluster shape on a spreading foot is a common form. $320–480

▲ INSCRIPTIONS
This late 19thC American mug by the Meridan Silver Co. bears a cartouche for an inscription and may be a christening mug. Beware of mugs on which the original inscription has been polished off to make way for new engraving. This makes the silver thin and prone to damage. Most collectible are christening mugs engraved with scenes from nursery rhymes. $220–350

TANKARDS

The earliest British tankards date from the mid-16thC, when very simple examples of earthenware, stoneware, or glass were made with silver mounts. Solid-silver tankards, decorated with engraved or chased designs of strapwork and fruit, were favored by the end of the century. In Germany large silver-gilt tankards were chased with biblical and mythological scenes, strapwork, masks, and flowers, and occasionally even decorated with coins. By the second half of the 17thC the most popular tankards were drum shaped with flat, molded bases, scroll handles, and simple, stepped covers. This form was succeeded in the 1730s by the baluster tankard. In the 19thC many plain tankards from earlier periods featured chased flowers and scrolls to suit the Victorian taste for elaborate and eclectic decoration.

◀ EARLY DESIGNS
This fine James II tankard of cylindrical form with a scroll handle and a flat stepped cover was produced in 1687 by the London maker Edward Gladwin and is typical of late 17thC English tankards. This simple shape was also produced in North America in the late 17thC with a similar volute thumbpiece, which was a speciality of New York silversmiths. Collectors should check that tankards are fully marked both on the bodies (usually on the upper part, near to the handle) and on the lids (either on the inside or near to the thumbpiece). $6,400–8,000

CHINOISERIE DECORATION
Chinoiserie decoration, which features Chinese-style motifs such as landscapes, pagodas, stunted trees, exotic birds, monsters, and figures, was enormously popular on French and English domestic silver from the late 17thC, largely as a result of to the expansion of trade between Europe and China. Designs were engraved or more commonly chased, as on this English tankard of 1684. Sometimes such decoration is a later addition. Chinoiserie decoration on silver is exceptionally rare and very collectible today. $40,000–64,000

Although this example is finely chased with chinoiserie decoration of figures and exotic birds, in general the decoration on tankards is very simple.

Check for tankards on which the original decoration has been removed. Tell-tale signs include traces of hammering and white marks on the surface of the metal.

Handles are usually only minimally decorated, possibly with motifs or rows of graduated beads.

Tankards may have been heavily used, so check for cracks, especially on vulnerable points around the handles.

► **LATER DECORATION**

This tankard from the 1690s has the stepped lid, scroll handle, and thumbpiece characteristic of late 17thC examples, and when originally made was probably very plain. Tankards such as this were often redecorated in the 19thC with Classical ornament of putti, fruiting vines, masks, shells, flowers, and grapes. While attractive, the later decoration diminishes the value. It was also common in the 19thC to convert tankards into jugs, which were thought to be more practical. Avoid conversions, as alterations lower the value and are illegal if the additions are not marked. $1,600–3,200

◄ **SCANDINAVIAN DESIGNS**

Late 17thC Scandinavian tankards stand on three ball feet, are embossed and chased with flowers, foliage, and scrolls and have pegs on the inside to set wagers for drinking games. This Norwegian tankard by Michael Olsen (*c*.1690) is engraved with names in a cartouche, and its cover is inset with a Dutch marriage medallion, suggesting that it was made for export and given as a wedding present. $9,600–12,800

► **"CYMRIC" SILVER**

Variations on the tankard form were many in the late 19th and early 20thC. This example, made in 1905 by the designer Archibald Knox for the "Cymric" silver range by the London firm of Liberty & Co., is embellished with a neo-Celtic design of swirling, interlaced tendrils, and cabochon-enamel decoration, hammered in low relief with a stylish lily-pad motif. Tankards such as this were rarely used, and were made for display only. $4,800–6,400

▲ **BALUSTER FORMS**

By the 1730s the baluster-form tankard, with a pronounced domed cover, double-scroll handle, and an applied plain or reeded band around the body, had become popular. Decoration was usually confined to an engraved armorial or a monogram. This example was made in 1739. $3,200–4,000

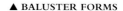

LIBERTY & CO. MARKS

Wares feature a Liberty & Co. mark and the range name beneath, but not the designer's name.

L & C

CYMRIC

BEAKERS, GOBLETS & CUPS

The basic cylindrical form of beakers has changed little since the 15thC. Most 16th and early 17thC beakers are plain, with bands of arabesques, stylized flowers, or foliage; later 17thC examples feature embossed-and-chased flowers and leaves, often with engraved initials or armorials. Lavishly engraved beakers were included in travelling sets with cutlery, spice boxes, and corkscrews. Silver goblets were made from the 16thC, but their production declined from the late 17thC until the late 18thC as vessels made of glass became more popular. There are many different types of cup, the most basic of which is the tumbler. Made from the mid-17thC, tumbler cups are of simple form with no feet or handles; most are plain except for heraldic engraving, initials, or inscriptions. As they are raised from heavy-gauge silver the weight of the metal is in the base so the cups returned to an upright position when knocked – this made them ideal for use by travelers at sea or in carriages. Other more complex designs include stirrup cups and wager cups, used for drinking games or toasts.

STIRRUP CUPS

Stirrup cups, which were first made in the 1770s, were used for making toasts at hunts and are sought after, especially if in pairs or large sets, or traceable to an actual hunt. Most, such as the example above (1787) by Smith & Sharp, are in the shape of a fox mask, although some are modeled as rabbit, stag, and horse heads. Marks are usually in a line around the neck. $8,000–9,600

▶ **WAGER CUPS**

This late 19thC Dutch wager cup is a copy of a late 16th or early 17thC design. Often found in Britain and The Netherlands, they were popularly used for drinking games or making toasts. The drinker would blow down a tube in the cup to make the sails spin and quickly drain the cup before the sails stopped or lose the bet. A rare 16thC wager cup would fetch 30 times the price of this example. $800–1,120

▶ **NOVELTIES**

Vessels in novelty forms were a popular concept in the Victorian and Edwardian periods. This little beaker, made in 1910, has been fashioned to resemble a sewing thimble, and (as inscribed) would have been used to measure a "thimbleful" of liquor. $240–320

LOVING CUPS

"Loving" cups are large vessels that were used for communal drinking at banquets and other festive gatherings. They have two or three handles, which enabled them to be passed easily from one guest to another. The term "loving" cup was commonplace during the 18thC.

◀ SILVER VERSUS GLASS

Goblets were rarely made from the late 17th until the end of the 18thC, when glass vessels for wine were more popular. In the Neo-classical period wine goblets were again made in silver, often in pairs, with minimally decorated vase-shaped ones especially notable. This vase-shaped wine goblet made in 1863 by Elkington & Co. is embossed with a battle scene (possibly a depiction of the Hundred Years War). $480–640

▶ KIDDUSH CUPS

Kiddush cups are goblets used in the Jewish community for drinking wine at religious ceremonies, on special occasions such as a wedding, or in the benediction before the evening meal preceding each Sabbath or a holy festival. These cups are usually are in the form of beakers or goblets and are often engraved with the Star of David (as on this small example of 1920) or Hebrew script. $95–160

ELKINGTON & CO.

In 1840 this Birmingham firm (est. *c*.1830) took out a patent for electroplating, which ensured the widespread use of the process and revolutionized the production of affordable silver plate. The mark (in various versions) is an abbreviation of the company name. **E&C°**

SETS AND PAIRS

From the 17thC, and particularly in continental Europe beakers were sometimes produced in sets, known as "nesting" sets, where the individual vessels fitted into one another for neat storage and protection. In the 18thC it was common for beakers, tumbler cups, and goblets to be made in pairs. Complete sets are most valuable; a pair will be worth more than twice the value of a single vessel. However, complete nesting sets are rare, and even pairs have usually been split up.

◀ LIQUOR TOTS

In pierced silver with cut-glass liners, liquor tots were usually made in boxed sets of six. They were especially popular in the late 19th and early 20thC – this example was made in 1896 – and often came with a matching silver-mounted decanter. A single liquor tot is worth little, but a set of six with its matching decanter would be very desirable. $640–800 (for a cased set of six)

Some of the most prestigious silver produced is associated with the bed-chamber. The status of the lady of the house was often reflected by silver made to adorn the dressing table – essential articles including toilet boxes for powders, soaps and lotions, bottles for perfume and cologne, comb and hairbrush sets, clothes brushes, and tiny boxes for pills and patches (fake beauty spots applied to the face by ladies of fashion in the 17th and 18thC). These pieces were produced in silver and silver gilt, sometimes with enameled decoration or featuring such exotic materials as tortoiseshell and mother-of-pearl. By the 19thC silver accessories were also made in sets. Initially the preserve of the very privileged, for whom many fine examples with highly ornate chased, engraved or embossed ornament were produced, by *c.*1830 dressing-table sets were also being made in simpler forms, aimed at a wider clientele and considered the zenith of gentility by the rising middle classes. From the late 19thC sets were also produced for men, typically with elegant, simply decorated silver accessories such as flasks to hold cologne. With the growth in travel for pleasure sparked by the success of the motor car, sets housed in protective, lockable wooden cases, intended specifically for use on the road, were also made. Also designed to adorn the dressing table, silver frames for mirrors and pictures are enduringly collectible: largely, as with much dressing-table silver, because many of them can still be used and enjoyed. Made in a range of eye-catching styles, toilet mirrors, heart-shaped mirrors, and double picture frames are especially sought after by collectors.

BOXES & BOTTLES

Although dressing-table silver is usually most valuable when sold as a matching set, the wide variety of decorative silver boxes and bottles intended to hold beauty products, toiletries and pharmaceutical items and to adorn the dressing table nevertheless forms an important collecting area. Not only do many accessories demonstrate imagination of form, decoration, and usage, as well as great inventiveness, they can also usually be acquired for modest sums and are easy to house and still very practical.

▲ **POWDER BOXES**
This powder box, made in Birmingham in 1910, features a pull-off *guilloché*-enameled silver lid and a glass base, and would originally have been part of a larger dressing-table set, which may also have included perfume bottles, jars, a hand mirror, shoehorn, button hook, and even a boudoir timepiece. The lids on boxes such as this usually featured mirrors on the insides and fitted tightly, so that the powder would not dry out. From *c.*1915 until the 1930s it was fashionable to decorate powder boxes with colored enamels. $110–150

MARKS
This mark is one of the later marks used by Mappin & Webb Ltd, appearing on 20thC wares. This mark is fairly easy to identify, being an abbreviation of the firm's name; but others, such as "JNM" (for John Newton Mappin) are less obvious.

M W
N B
&

▲ PILL BOXES

Little boxes were used from medieval times until the late 18thC to hold beauty patches, which ladies of fashion applied to their faces, thus coining the name "patchbox". Such dainty boxes as this pale-blue *champlevé* enamel example with a detachable lid, made in 1925, are still popularly used to hold items as diverse as pills, mints, and powder. $160–190

▼ DUAL-PURPOSE BOTTLES

This bright-cut glass bottle, made *c*.1780, was probably used to hold patches or powder as well as perfume. Most bottles of this type were made in France and often bear only a duty mark; however, some examples were made in the late 18thC in Birmingham. Watch out for inexpensive boxes of this type, which may be of base metal rather than silver. $960–1,120

ENAMELING

Wares decorated with enameling should be carefully checked to ensure that the enamel has not been chipped or restored, as this will considerably lower the value of the piece.

MARKS

From 1868 Gorham Manufacturing Co. (est. 1818) of Providence, Rhode Island marked its wares with a date letter or symbol and the firm's trademark.

► NOVELTY SHAPES

Novelty scent bottles in the forms of musical instruments, furniture, sedan chairs, and carriages were made in large numbers from *c*.1890 until 1900, especially in Germany and, as in this 19thC embossed example, The Netherlands. The shapes were stamped in several parts on large sheets of silver, cut out, and soldered together, but the parts do not always match. These bottles should bear English import marks of *c*.1900 – 18thC marks are spurious. $700–770

◄ ITEMS FOR MEN

In the 19thC it became fashionable for men to scent themselves with cologne. Edwardian toilet sets for men often held silver accessories, such as this satin-finished flask of *c*.1906 by Gorham, brushes, shaving items and perhaps also curling tongs for the moustache. $160–800

DRESSING-TABLE SETS

Dressing-table sets, sometimes fitted in wooden traveling cases, were made throughout the 19th and early 20thC. They succeed the earlier lavish toilet sets that from the late 17thC were essential luxuries for noblewomen and very often given to them by their husbands to commemorate their marriage or the birth of an heir. The essential accessories of a dressing-table set were a hand mirror and hairbrushes, backed with silver; perfume bottles or flasks with silver mounts, clothes brushes, combs, and shoehorns were often also included. Larger sets may also have contained eye-baths, jewel caskets, pomade jars, and even drinking cups, and some elaborate examples featured secret compartments. Made of silver or silver gilt, these items were often either embossed or enameled, and then engraved with initals or a monogram. It is important to check that all the pieces in a set are by the same maker and match exactly. Prices vary according to the number of items in a set, the extent of the decoration and the condition.

▶ **19THC**
TRAVELING SETS
This parcel-gilt, velvet-lined set, made in 1844 by R. & S. Garrard & Co., is a fine example of the portable sets that were in vogue in the 19thC. By the 1830s such sets were no longer confined to the dressing table of a lady's chamber and range from the simple to the highly sumptuous. $11,200–16,000

▲ **EARLY 20THC**
TRAVELING SETS
Ladies' traveling sets such as this one from the 1920s, fitted in an elegant crocodile-skin case, tend to be more popular among today's collectors than the larger, more lavish examples. Traveling boxes usually came with outer canvas covers to protect the exotic wood or leather from wear and tear. $2,400–2,880

MARKS
Garrard has been a dominant name in the silver trade since the 18thC, with Robert Garrard I and his son Robert Garrard II particularly influential. Due mainly to the direction of the latter, the family firm was appointed Goldsmith to the Crown in 1830 and, in 1843, Crown Jewelers. This mark was used from 1822 until 1900, but wares made since 1900 feature the initials "RG" only. In 1963 Garrard & Co. merged with Mappin & Webb Ltd and Elkington & Co. to form British Silverware Ltd.

▶ **SETS FOR MEN**
From the 19thC silver toilet sets for gentlemen were not uncommon, although they were always smaller and not as elaborate as those for women, and for personal use rather than show. They were usually housed in fitted cases and were essential accessories when traveling by the newly popular motor car. The scent bottles are generally plain, with very simple decoration, as shown by the three cologne bottles in the leather traveling box featured right. Made *c*.1920, these bottles have glass stoppers fitted within silver screw tops. $640–720

◀ **POPULAR GIFTS**
Small silver sets for the dressing table such as this one decorated with gold-colored enamel (1940) were popular presents for young women coming of age. Many found today are of fine quality and good value for money, although those that have been used extensively may be quite worn. Watch out for damage to the enamel and check that an engraved monogram has not been removed, which leaves the silver very thin. Sets in good condition, fitted in a pretty, lined box, will be most highly priced. $400–800

WELL-KNOWN NAMES
Dressing-table silver by a celebrated maker such as Bernard Instone is extremely collectible and commands a high price today. These sets are made of very high-quality, heavy-gauge silver and typically show close attention to detail, for example through the use of exotic materials or elaborate decoration such as hand-hammering seen on the mirror handle (1925) shown here. $3,520–4,000

MIRRORS & PICTURE FRAMES

Most silver frames found today are small, relatively affordable and date from the 1880s and later. Produced in a host of styles and forms – from imposing Classical to naturalistic Art Nouveau and geometric Art Deco – they are very popular, being both decorative and functional. On most examples the silver has been stamped from a sheet and is consequently extremely thin and easily damaged. Better-quality pieces are cast. High-quality silver-framed mirrors are rare and very keenly sought after by collectors. The largest examples tend to command the highest prices, with heart-shaped mirrors particularly favored. Late 17th and 18thC mirrors are rare. Smaller than frames made for mirrors, picture frames also come in a variety of desirable styles, with double picture frames especially popular. The mount, velvet backing, and strut should all be in good condition, and modern reproductions, where the pattern is weakly stamped out of thin metal, should be avoided. With American frames, be suspicious if you encounter English marks, as they are usually fake.

◀ TOILET MIRRORS
Toilet mirrors for both ladies and gentlemen were originally designed for traveling, and the earliest examples from the late 17thC and the Queen Anne period were fitted in boxes along with such necessities as bottles, combs, brushes, and toilet boxes. The easel-back support allowed the mirror to stand upright, thus making it easier to consult when washing, shaving or powdering. This cartouche-shaped toilet mirror was made in the late 19thC by the French maker Bointaburet and is decorated with a border of shells and bulrushes. Several reputed French silversmiths, such as Cardheillac, Jean-Baptiste Claude Odiot, and, later, Jean Puiforcat made similar high-quality toilet mirrors, which are usually very highly priced. $3,200–4,800

BEWARE
It is important to buy a mirror that has not been restored, so check carefully to see that all parts of the mirror are original. Remove the mount and ensure that the original glass with its bevelled edge is still in place, even if it has been permanently discolored or spotted. Replaced wooden backing and new velvet or leather covering will also reduce the value.

▶ HEART-SHAPED MIRRORS
This late Victorian mirror by the English silversmith William Comyns is delicately stamped and pierced with flowers, trailing vines, scrolls, cherubs, winged figures, and masks. Heart-shaped mirrors in good condition, with fine-quality bevelled glass and highly ornate decoration, are particularly valuable. The large size (height: 18in/45cm) and lavish decoration of this mirror ensure it will fetch a high price, even though many similar examples were made. $1,280–1,920

◀ PHOTOGRAPHY

In the 1880s the invention of cameras aimed specifically at the amateur photographer and the development of roll-film, which made it easier to take several pictures at one time, made photography accessible to a far wider audience. Frames were created in hundreds of different designs in standard sizes, to meet the demand for an appropriate place to display these recorded images. This oval frame, made in Birmingham in 1905, still features its original bevelled-glass plate and wooden easel back. It has been embossed with Art Nouveau-style decoration of dragonflies, butterflies, and flowers typical of the period from *c*.1890 to *c*.1920. $640–800

▶ FRAME QUALITY

Picture frames contain very little silver, and frequent polishing over time leaves many in a damaged condition; such examples, particularly plain oblong ones with little or no decoration, should be avoided. Also watch out for frames that have been fitted at a later date with a mirror – these conversions are easy to spot, as all frames have detachable backs held on with swivel clips. This example, made in 1900, is decorated with trailing flowers and stylized anthemion in the Art Nouveau taste. $320–400

▲ COLLECTIBILITY

Although the velvet-covered card backing makes this picture frame of 1902, with its decoration of pierced lily leaves and flowers, less valuable than if it had a wooden back, this delicate example is nevertheless well made and collectible. Picture frames are very popular with collectors as they are both practical and decorative. Double picture frames are particularly sought after. $640–800

◀ AMERICAN DESIGNS

Picture frames are popularly collected in the USA. Although the low-relief etched and chased decoration on this 20thC example has been carried out by machine, it is nonetheless of good quality. If picture frames still have their original glass, check the latter at the corners to ensure it is not chipped. Better-quality frames feature bevelled glass. $400–480

A vast assortment of fine writing accessories is available on the market, offering limitless opportunities for assembling a varied, affordable collection. Although the written word has long played a vital role in communication, early writing equipment is extremely rare and found mainly in museums. However, as more sophisticated methods of communication developed from the late 18thC, including the establishment of the "penny" post and the use envelopes, and as letter-writing and the keeping of journals came into vogue, the fashion for practical yet decorative desk furnishings resulted in the production of an abundance of writing equipment. From decorative silver inkstands, produced with matching accessories, to inkwells and such portable writing sets intended for travel as penners, a wide range of items is available. Pens, including dip pens, fountain pens, and ballpoint pens, and pencils, which were also produced in quantity, have become increasingly sought after among collectors since the mid-1980s. Dip pens were the most widely used type of pen until ink-flow systems that facilitated a smooth flow of ink to the nib became standard in fountain pens from the late 19thC. Blotters, stamp holders, seals, brushes, and wipes for cleaning pens, paper knives and rulers are only some of the diverse miscellaneous writing accessories available. Many such items can be easily repaired and restored, and can therefore still be used and enjoyed today, which is central to their appeal.

INKSTANDS

Few inkstands were made before the end of the 17thC. The earliest examples are in the form of a rectangular casket, with an inkpot, a wafer pot (for wax disks for sealing letters), and a pounce pot for sand or pounce, which was sprinkled on parchment paper to prevent the ink from spreading. They gained popularity from the 18thC when examples were made of silver, Sheffield plate, and sometimes pewter. Most inkstands from this time were in the form of a footed tray, usually with a trough for pens and perhaps also a bell, a waxjack, or a taperstick.

▲ "STANDISHES"
By the 18thC most inkstands consisted of an oblong silver tray on four feet, usually with an inkpot (shown left, with small holes in the rim to hold quill pens) and a pounce pot (right), plus a taperstick or a small handbell. Early inkstands were often known by the name "standish", after their upwardly curved or dished sides. Most early examples are plain, except for molded scroll-and-shell or beaded rims and fancy feet. The engraved armorial of this inkstand (1720) probably mean it was commissioned by a gentleman. $16,000–24,000

INSCRIPTIONS
Many inkstands bear inscriptions, coats-of-arms, or armorials, which can provide clues to the identities of the original owners. An important provenance will add to the value.

◀ **18THC INKSTANDS**
Early 18thC inkstands tend to be well made and more valuable than later ones. Inkpots were often fitted with ceramic or lead liners, but these have usually been lost, as have the bells (used to call servants when a fresh supply of parchment was needed and to hide a pile of wafers or wax) and covers. Complete examples in top condition such as this one from 1730 are very desirable. $9,600–12,000

▶ **NEW TECHNIQUES**
Mechanization in the 1770s sparked a surge in the popularity of items that could be mass produced from a small amount of silver. This inkstand (1780) features a box with a lid in the form of a chamberstick for melting sealing wax and a recess for pens.

The silver-mounted glass ink bottles (introduced in the mid-18thC) were a cheaper alternative to all-silver ones. Watch out for unmarked fittings (such as snuffers, lids, and guard rails for glass bottles), as they may be replacements. $2,400–4,000

◀ **VICTORIAN DESIGNS**
This late Victorian gallery inkstand by George Fox is a copy of one made in the 1760s, although it is larger in size. The cast feet and border have been separately applied, and the very delicate piercing of the gallery was finished by hand. The taperstick lifts off to reveal a well for small seals, stamps, or nibs, and there is a depression for holding pens. This example features two inkwells for differently colored inks. All separate parts should be marked. $3,200–4,800

▶ **EDWARDIAN INKSTANDS**
This Edwardian inkstand of 1902 is in a popular style that was produced using an economy of silver. The border has been machine stamped, and is therefore very light and flimsy. By this date many 18thC writing accoutrements, such as pounce pots and sealing wax, were no longer features of inkstands. Novelty examples featuring items in the form of figures or animals were also popular at this time. $1,120–1,600

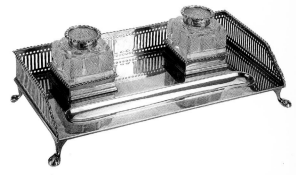

INKWELLS, PENNERS, PENS & PENCILS

Few silver inkwells survive from before the first half of the 17thC; until the 18thC they were usually made portable so that they could be used by traveling scribes. Some inkwells were made in sets, or contained within penners – portable writing kits, made from the 17thC, that were ideal for use when traveling. Silver pens and pencils have also long been made in a range of decorative designs. From the 1840s the dip pen was the most common writing instrument,

and many silver dip pens were made, including some examples that were part of desk sets or that had separate stands or trays. The fountain pen, which contains its own reservoir of ink, was first mentioned by the diarist Samuel Pepys in 1663, and thereafter produced in an array of imaginative styles. Silver pencils were made by silversmiths, who bought the internal mechanisms and produced fitted pencil cases, as well as by large specialist manufacturers.

◀ CAPSTAN FORMS
This inkwell (1907) in the shape of a ship's capstan (over which a tie-up rope was thrown) was a common form and very popular from the 1880s until the 1920s; it remains in great demand among collectors today. Many examples were made as parts of boxed sets, sometimes with

matching candlesticks. Many capstan inkwells had elaborate lids or, as here, hinged covers with channels to hold dip pens, and glass liners inside to facilitate cleaning. Made of very thin sheet silver and loaded for added stability, this inkwell is susceptible to damage such as thinning, denting and creasing, which would greatly reduce its value. $240–320

▶ NOVELTY INKWELLS
Silver inkwells were produced in a variety of imaginative and decorative designs, often in combination with other materials. Some were made as special commissions, and were intended for display only. This example (1840) by the Birmingham maker Joseph

Wilmore features an opaque-glass bottle, with a hand-formed silver frame of graduated lily leaves, which have been separately stamped out and soldered to the stem. Novelty inkwells such as this are very popular. $1,120–1,440

◀ DESK SETS
This desk set comprises a cut-glass inkwell with a hinged cover, a matching paper holder, a dip pen, and a desk seal engraved in intaglio with a crest and motto. Made in 1905, this set would originally have been fitted in a lined case; it bears English import marks and was probably made in Austria or Switzerland. $960–1,280

PENNERS

Penners consist of a tubular shaft for holding a short quill with an inkwell at one end, that was often stuffed with wool to absorb the ink and reduce leakage, and a pounce holder at the other.

They are very collectible, especially such fine examples as this French silver-mounted shagreen one. Less-valuable penners were made c.1800 in Birmingham by makers such as Joseph Taylor and Samuel Pemberton. $4,000–4,800

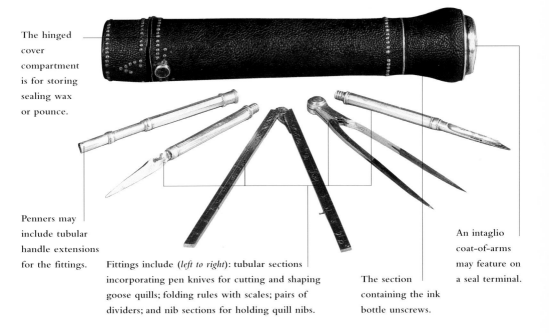

The hinged cover compartment is for storing sealing wax or pounce.

Penners may include tubular handle extensions for the fittings.

Fittings include (*left to right*): tubular sections incorporating pen knives for cutting and shaping goose quills; folding rules with scales; pairs of dividers; and nib sections for holding quill nibs.

The section containing the ink bottle unscrews.

An intaglio coat-of-arms may feature on a seal terminal.

◀ DIP PENS

Dip pens were the most common type of writing instrument from 1840 until the late 19thC. Elaborately decorated versions were produced as symbols of wealth and incorporated such techniques as filigree, repoussé, niello, and engraving. Examples bearing makers' marks, such as this elegant early 20thC American pen by the Gorham Manufacturing Co., are particularly sought after by collectors. $130–225

◀ FOUNTAIN PENS

Fountain pens have been made since the 17thC, but most surviving examples date from the late 19thC. This fine-quality example by the British penmaker MacNiven & Cameron features the firm's trademark curved Waverly nib and is quite rare and very collectible. The quality and originality of the decoration, the maker, and the quality and size of the nib determine the value of these pens. $320–400

◀ PENCILS

Many elaborate novelty pencils were made by leading jewelers as special commissions, and these can be very valuable. This silver repoussé pencil with a twist extension was made by Hicks of New York. Other notable makers of pencils include Butler, Fairchild, and Sampson Mordan & Co. By the mid-19thC retractable examples that could be attached to *châtelaines* (ornamental clasps) had come into fashion. $160–320

MISCELLANEOUS

Completing formal documents or letters and dispatching them was, until fairly recently, a protracted process, involving a range of equipment. Desk accessories designed to help with letter-writing include blotters used for absorbing ink and preventing it from smudging and stamp holders for storing stamps, often in quirky novelty forms. Until the introduction of the "penny" post in the 19thC, the cost of sending a letter was based on its weight, and it was usual to fold letters upon themselves and secure them using melted wax.

Accessories designed for this purpose include sealing-stick holders made for holding and protecting blocks of wax – sometimes with built-in tapers – and seals, which were typically branded with the sender's monogram or crest and pressed into the melted wax that was dripped onto the paper. Knives for opening letters or turning the pages of large illustrated books, so as not to soil the pages, were also produced in silver in a host of innovative designs. These accessories form a diverse and often affordable category of collectibles.

▶ BLOTTERS

As ink was slow to dry on oily vellum, poor-quality uncoated paper was commonly used for blotting in the 18thC alongside powder or pounce; however, it was not until the early 1840s that it was sold specifically as "blotting paper". On this modern blotter (1919) absorbent paper is wrapped around the wooden base and then tucked under the detachable silver top. Decorated with a yachting pennant, this blotter was probably part of a larger desk set used on a boat or ship. Blotters are popular with collectors, although condition is vital and frequent use has rendered many of them worthless. $240–320

◀ STAMP HOLDERS

Stamp holders were made in a huge variety of shapes and sizes, often with a postal theme such as envelope-shaped pockets. Some were made in novelty forms such as this tiny chest-of-drawers (1911), which features four separate compartments, by the Birmingham maker Saunders & Shepherd. These small dainty items are quirky and can be very valuable. $640–800

◀ NOVELTIES

Other collectible novelty stamp holders include this American silver pencil containing a stamp roll (1900) and the silver pouch (*see* below), which holds stamps of two different sizes. Pencil and stamp holder $160–190; pouch $60–80

◀ SEALING STICKS

As the sticks of wax used to seal documents were brittle, they were often kept in protective tubes with slider mechanisms for pushing out the wax. This silver sealing stick, made in 1895, has an extendable taper mounted alongside with which to melt the wax and is typical of the late Victorian fancy for gadgets. This example has been made from a thin sheet of silver; any damage would reduce its value. $190–225

▲ SEALS AND WAX

Until the practice of sending letters in envelopes became widespread, letters were commonly sealed using wax and branded with a seal bearing the crest of the sender. This silver-and-ivory example of 1865, showing the owner's monogram, was made by the London firm of Sampson Mordan & Co. Prior to the 19thC, sealing wax was a combination of beeswax and resin, and it was dyed either red with vermilion or green with verdigris. Thereafter a mix of vermilion and shellac was used. $125–160

▶ FOB AND NOVELTY SEALS

Fob seals, such as the silver-gilt example on a gold chain of 1840 shown here, were one of the range of seal types made principally for men. Engraved with monograms or crests, they were suspended from chains attached to waistcoats. Other types of seal include ring seals with the seal in the signet of the ring, finial seals attached to the ends of pencils, pens, sealing-wax holders, and even spoons, and seals that were worn suspended from *châtelaines* or watch chains. $480–640

◀ PAPER KNIVES

Many large paper knives were made in the shape of swords or scimitars, such as this example with a thick ivory blade and fluted silver handle; they were often used for turning the pages of a book. The smaller knife – made at the beginning of the 20thC and of Austro-Hungarian origin – is decorated with a silver eagle's head with glass eyes and has an ebony blade; it was probably used as a bookmark. Novelty paper knives are desirable, as are lavishly decorated examples with intricate handles. Large knife: $480–800; small knife: $400–480

In 16thC France, snuff – pulverized tobacco taken by both men and women and sniffed up the nose – was considered beneficial to the health, and the custom of taking it was introduced to Britain a century later. Small boxes for storing snuff were made in the early 18thC, from simple engine-turned designs to lavish examples featuring embossed or enameled decoration of battles or hunting scenes. However, by the mid-19thC the popularity of snuff had waned as cigar and cheroot smoking became fashionable, and few snuff boxes were produced after this date. The Spanish had introduced cigars to Europe shortly after the discovery of the Americas in 1492, but the first European cigar factory only opened in Hamburg in 1788. In Britain, the taste for cigar smoking was well established by the end of the 18thC. From the end of the 19thC, cigarettes became very fashionable, and their popularity was accompanied by the production of cigarette cases. Throughout the 19th and 20thC Birmingham manufacturers produced a wide variety of smoking accessories, from cigar boxes to vesta cases for matches, which were known as "vestas". After World War I cigarette smoking became increasingly fashionable, and silver cigarette cases were carried or stylishly worn like a piece of elegant jewelry. Many examples are extremely decorative, and although highly elaborate cigarettte cases made by such reputed jewelers as Fabergé can still fetch a premium, most cases are fairly affordable, making this a popular area of collecting. Novelty lighters and cigar or cigarette cutters are also popular.

SNUFF BOXES

Silver boxes to hold ready-rubbed snuff were made from the beginning of the 18thC. The development of mechanical techniques in the late 18thC guaranteed a plentiful supply of inexpensive sheet silver from which snuff boxes could be manufactured to meet the growing demand. Large "table snuff" boxes were used after dinner, when a host would offer his guests snuff from a communal box. By the mid-19thC the fashion for taking snuff had waned, and production declined.

▲ NIELLO WORK
Niello is an ancient decorative technique where an amalgam of lead, copper, sulphur, and silver is used to fill engraved decoration, as seen on this fine Russian snuff box (1839) decorated with an architectural scene. The quality of the engraved detail, the condition of the niello and the presence of hallmarks will be crucial to the value. Some of the finest niello snuff boxes were produced in the region of Velikiy Ustyug in Russia; they are typically decorated with townscapes, architectural scenes or floral designs, and are sought after by collectors. $800–1,120

IDENTIFICATION
Snuff boxes are distinguished from other small boxes by the lip tucked under the lid on the interior, which helps to keep the snuff dry and prevents spillage.

A.J. STRACHAN

The silversmith Alexander James Strachan (*d.c.*1845) is especially noted for his production of small objects such as snuff boxes. Wares should bear his mark as shown below.

A·J·S

◀ INSCRIPTIONS

Many snuff boxes feature engraved initials, presentation inscriptions or coats-of-arms, as on the central shield of this silver-plated example (1850), which was probably owned by a member of a fraternity. Large snuff boxes were often commissioned from such makers as A.J. Strachan and Nathaniel Mills and made as presentation gifts. $160–240

▶ FETES GALANTES

This late 19thC snuff box copies a late 18thC design. Of Swiss origin, it has been decorated with enamels and inset with a miniature of a scene known as a *fête galante* – made famous by the 18thC French painter Jean-Antoine Watteau. A fine-quality copy of an original 18thC design, this snuff box is surprisingly affordable. $640–800

▲ SNUFF MULL

Known as a snuff mull – the name "mull" is dialect for "mill", and some snuff mulls featured devices for mashing snuff – this typically Scottish design (1830) has been fashioned from ram's horn and decorated with silver mounts and a domed cover inset with amethyst quartz. Snuff mulls made of ram's horn usually date from between 1790 and 1840, and are very often unmarked. Marked provincial examples are rare and therefore sought after. $320–400

▼ GOOD CONDITION

Snuff boxes such as this example (1820s), which features applied engine-turned decoration on the cover and gilding inside, were made in vast numbers in the early 19thC. Good condition is vital. For top value the hinged cover should fit snugly and be airtight, and the engraving should be sharp and undamaged. $480–640

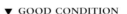

VESTA CASES

Vesta cases were made to house friction matches, which were invented *c.*1840 and known from the late 19thC as "vestas" after the Roman goddess of the hearth. These small cases were initally adapted from snuff boxes, with the addition of serrated strikers. As smoking became increasingly fashionable from the late 19thC, small rectangular boxes with rounded corners and closely fitting hinged lids – vital to prevent matches from combusting – were popularly made specifically for vestas. They were produced in a wide variety of shapes, with engraved, chased, or enameled decoration. From *c.*1890 Birmingham was the major center of production of vesta cases in Britain, although the very highest-quality workmanship is usually found on London-made cases. Some vesta cases have double compartments for matches, or were combined with other objects such as pen knives, cigar cutters, or stamp holders. From the late 19thC novelty examples were produced in great numbers. With the introduction of the more durable petrol lighter the production of vesta cases stopped after World War I.

▶ **EROTICA**
Many vesta cases made in the late Victorian and Edwardian periods were enameled with nudes seated or reclining in erotic poses, as on this example of 1904. Providing a welcome diversion for a naughty gentleman while lighting his pipe, these risqué designs adorn some of the most highly treasured vestas. $480–800

▲ ▶ **ANIMAL FORMS**
Some of the most common novelty vesta cases are in the form of birds and animals such as the "fish" (1900) and plated "owl" with glass inset eyes (1890s) shown here. The head of the "owl" tilts back on a hinge. It is a high-quality London-made vesta case and would be sought after among collectors. Fish: $320–400; owl: $160–240

▼ **SPORTING THEMES**
This vesta case (1920s) in the form of a golf ball would no doubt appeal to golfing enthusiasts as well as to collectors of vesta cases. The lid is hinged at the top for easy closure, and has a loop for suspension from a silver chain. The flattened round shape means that this case would neatly slip into the pocket. $320–640

▶ NOVELTY VESTA CASES

Novelty vesta cases such as this *trompe l'oeil* example (*c.*1900) in the form of a rolled-up newspaper with an enameled "stamp" were produced in the USA in great numbers between 1890 and 1910. The interiors were often gilded to prevent the phosphorous match heads from reacting with the silver. $640–800

◀ PICTORIAL VESTA CASES

Pictorial cases such as this example featuring the popular characters Mr Punch and his dog Toby are great rarities and extremely valuable. The finest examples are usually enameled (as here), although others are chased or engraved. Fine pictorial vesta cases were a speciality of makers such as Sampson Mordan & Co. and Henry William Dee. $8,000–11,200

◀ SETS

This unusually large (3in/7.5cm) vesta case (1903) was made in London by Sampson Mordan & Co. This popular design, made as part of a series with each enameled soldier representing a different regiment, was first produced in the late 19thC. Cases from this series feature very fine enameling and are highly prized and valuable. $3,200–4,800

◀ ART NOUVEAU

The major exponent of the Art Nouveau style in the USA was Tiffany & Co., who inspired the mass-production of such designs as this stamped example of *c.*1900. The sensuous nymph and naturalistic imagery are typical Art Nouveau motifs. The serrated edge at the base is for striking matches. $95–130

SAMPSON MORDAN & CO.

This London firm – famed for its pens, pencils and novelty and character wares – entered its first mark in the 1820s.

CIGAR & CIGARETTE CASES

As a result of the increased popularity of smoking in the late 19thC, cigar and cigarette cases were produced in great numbers. They were made in two forms: either as boxes for storing cigars and cigarettes at home or as portable carrying cases. Early cigarette cases are small, as cigarettes made before *c.*1900 did not have filters and were consequently shorter than those manufactured today. Many portable examples are oblong, with rounded sides and corners, and are characteristically slim or curved to fit comfortably inside a pocket. Enameled cigarette cases featuring battle scenes, aircraft, and animals are among the most sought after by collectors, although in general those decorated with naughty erotic scenes tend to achieve the highest prices.

◀ **CIGAR CASES**
This Russian case with a pull-off cap was designed to hold a small bundle of cheroots or cigars and would fit comfortably inside a pocket. These cigar cases were made in great numbers in the mid-19thC and were embellished in a variety of decorative techniques, from embossed hunting scenes to enameled and elegant engraved designs. The ancient technique of niello, which enjoyed a revival in the 19thC, has been used to decorate this example. $640–960

▶ **CIGARETTE CASES**
This cigarette case (1925), which has been enameled with *trompe l'oeil* decoration to simulate a packet of cigarettes, is typical of early 20thC designs. It comes with a matching vesta case. $960–1,280

▼ **EXCLUSIVE DESIGNS**
After World War I cigarette smoking became fashionable among the wealthy, and elaborate silver cigarette cases, such as this spectacular tube-shaped example (1915) set with a rose-diamond thumbpiece, were made for ladies to carry on special occasions. This example was designed by the Russian goldsmith and jeweler Carl Fabergé and is extremely desirable. $3,000–5,000

FABERGE MARK
Under the direction of Carl Fabergé (1846–1920) the Fabergé firm in Saint Petersburg became one of the world's most renowned jewelers. As shown, designs are marked "KF" or "K. Fabergé" in Cyrillic letters.

◀ ART DECO

This fine-quality cigarette case, decorated in the Art Deco style with bold, bright colors and a stark geometric design, typifies the exuberant examples produced in the 1920s and 1930s. This case was possibly made in continental Europe and would originally have been fairly expensive. $480–640

COLLECTING

Late 19th and early 20thC cigarette cases do not fit modern cigarettes, and unless the cases are jeweled or made of an especially valuable material, in general – as with vesta cases – they are not especially popular among today's collectors.

▶ SINGLE CIGAR CASES

This unusual Birmingham torpedo-shaped case (1902) was intended to hold a single cigar and fit neatly into a jacket pocket. Holders for two or three cigars were also made. Cases such as this, with elegant decoration, are highly prized. $320–480

◀ CIGARETTE BOX

Fine-quality silver cigar and cigarette boxes for the table or desk, such as this very handsome London-made example (1928) with a sprung handle, had wooden or solid-silver bases, whereas less-valuable examples are usually lined in the base with pieces of leather that are "loaded" and lined with cedar wood to keep the contents fresh. Today these boxes are often converted for use as jewelry boxes, lined with velvet. $1,440–1,600

▶ FAMOUS SMOKERS

This late 1970s parcel-gilt cigar box by Stuart Devlin has a flat base, wooden liner, and flat silver top. It has been embossed with scenes depicting the life of Sir Winston Churchill, whose celebrated fondness for cigars makes him an appropriate subject. $960–1,280

MISCELLANEOUS

The custom of retiring for a smoke after a meal became fashionable among gentlemen from the mid-19thC, reaching its peak of popularity between 1880 and 1910. Cigars and cheroots were an expensive luxury to be savoured, and as a result considerable ceremony was attached to their preparation and enjoyment. Items produced to enhance the pleasure of the smoking ritual include cigar cutters, which were sometimes made in combination with other forms, for example with chambersticks, or with storage for vestas; lighters, which notably were usually non-portable and designed to stand on a table; and combination "companions", which were used to perform a range of tasks by the smoker. Especially favored were novelty designs, which remain popular with collectors today.

> ### LIGHTERS
> Novelty lighters were often lightly constructed, poorly made and prone to damage. As a result they are fairly rare in good condition

▲ NOVELTY LIGHTERS
The front section of this gondola lighter (1906) is for holding spirit oil and also features a nozzle for a wick, so that the lighter could be used at a table. Matches could be stored in the hollow section of the hull, and the deck-house opens to reveal a match striker. $3,200–4,800

▶ MULTI-PURPOSE DESIGNS
Cigar cutters in the form of chambersticks, such as this example of 1896, were popular from the late 19thC. The pan is intended for collecting ashes, spent matches and cuttings, the nozzle is to hold a candle, and the attached tubular cutter is for cutting cigars. $960–1,120

◀ NOVELTIES
Dragon-shaped table lighters such as this silver-plate-and-antelope-horn example (1900) by Walker & Hall were often found in late Victorian regimental silver. They were made, usually in pairs, for handing around the table. $560–720

◀ CIGAR CUTTERS
On this early 20thC cutter, made in 1912, the cigar is inserted into the opening on the central pole, which has a metal cutter inside that snips off the end of the cigar when the top section is pressed down. The heart-shaped base could be used as an ashtray and receptacle for discarded clippings; the tubular container attached to the back is intended for holding bundles of matches. $400–560

SMOKERS' COMPANIONS

The angular form and red-blue-and-white champlevé enameling featured on this smoker's companion, made in 1878, is highly characteristic of "Pan Slavic" designs, which were produced in Russia in the late 19thC. High-quality, superbly executed smoking accessories such as this unusual example are keenly sought after by wealthy cigar-smoking collectors and achieve a high price on the market today. $6,400–8,000

The angular handle makes the companion easy to carry from room to room or pass around the table.

The taperstick is used for igniting tobacco and lighting the room.

The "guillotine" is used for snipping off the ends of cigars.

Watch out for chipped enameling.

The hollow body of the vessel could be used to store cigars, cigarettes, and cheroots, or serve as an ashtray.

Two small containers, one on each side, with hinged lids and ball finials are for containing vestas or small tapers.

The diverse range of small silver pieces featured in this section offers great scope to collectors, especially to those on limited budgets. Topics covered include sewing accessories, pomanders and vinaigrettes, card cases, nursery ware, buckles, sovereign holders, timepieces, toothbrush sets, and lamps. Sewing equipment, such as thimbles, pincushions, tape measures, ribbon threaders, and scissors, is highly sought after today. Indeed some auction houses have sales that are devoted exclusively to these items, and societies and clubs for collectors have been established both in Britain and the USA. Pomanders are scented balls, sometimes made in silver and intended to counter foul odours and prevent fainting fits. They were superseded from the late 18th by vinaigrettes – dainty boxes fitted with grilles, which held in place sponges soaked in aromatic vinegar. Cases for holding visiting cards are popular, and many examples displaying great inventiveness and craftsmanship are available at affordable prices. Such small objects as these are also easy to house, which is of major importance to many collectors. Nursery items, many of which were made to celebrate the christening of a child, include bowl-and-spoon sets, characteristically in silk-lined fitted cases, mugs decorated with such favorite childhood themes as nursery rhymes and letters of the alphabet, silver spoons, typically bearing the initials or dates of birth of the children for whom they were originally made, and decorative rattles. Also covered is a selection of unclassifiable items, from buckles and posy holders to silver tongue-scrapers and toothbrush sets.

SEWING ACCESSORIES I

Many sewing accessories were made at least partly of silver, often in imaginative designs and with detailed decoration. Among the most collectible items are *étuis* (tiny sets containing personal items and often including accessories for sewing), thimbles, and novelties. These small decorative silver items were not usually intended for professional seamstresses, who instead used less-precious, more durable tools.

▲ MINIATURE ETUIS
This *étui* (1¾in/4.5cm) comprises a tape measure, thimble, and, hidden beneath the thimble, a row of bobbins. The good condition of the filigree work, together with an early date (*c*.1800), makes this example very collectible. $480–800

▼ TAPE MEASURES
This charming silver-plated American tape measure is inscribed with the words "Pull my head but not my leg", and the head pulls out to reveal a tape measure. American silversmiths excelled in the production of such novelties. $800–1,120

◀ ETUIS

A small ornamented case fitted with a variety of tiny implements, the *étui* (French for "case") provided ready access to personal items deemed crucial to running a household such as scissors, needles, tweezers, thimbles, bodkins, and pencils. Often hung from *châtelaines* (clasps worn at the waist from two or more chains or clips), these cases were made in a range of shapes, and often decorated with enamels and gilding. For top value, an *étui* should be complete with its original contents, as exemplified by this French, ivory example (1870s). $400–560

◀ AMERICAN THIMBLES

Thimbles are popular among collectors in both Britain and the USA. This example, which was produced during the 1920s, features the time-honoured adage "A Stitch in Time Saves Nine". $320–400

◀ COMBINATIONS

Sometimes different sewing accessories were combined in one design, such as this needlecase, bobbin, holder and thimble set (1790). In some examples the circular foot unscrews to reveal a tiny spike, which was used as a stiletto for piercing material. The end was sometimes engraved with initials or a monogram and used as a seal. $960–1,280

▲ MARKS

This thimble (1892), which features a matching velvet-lined, chained holder, was probably intended to be hung from a *châtelaine*. Unusually, a tiny set of hallmarks is hidden in the decoration – on some thimbles there is not sufficient room for hallmarks. $95–110

◀ SCISSORS

Small pairs of scissors for fine trimming work such as these ones (1889) were made as part of sewing sets, to be hung from *châtelaines* or fitted into their own lined cases. Many British examples were manufactured in Sheffield, as the blades were usually made of steel. The handles were typically of "loaded" hollow silver. Some scissors were made with protective silver sheathes. $240–300

SEWING ACCESSORIES II

Indispensable items for sewing that can be found in silver include pincushions, ribbon threaders, and hemming gauges. Pincushions, used for keeping pins, needles, and decorative hatpins or hairpins safe, often feature "loaded" (weighted) sheet-silver bases and velvet-covered padded tops and are typically in novelty forms. Ribbon threaders were used as an aid to weaving ribbons through garments and were also often made in novelty forms.

Châtelaines, which originated in the 17thC, are decorative clasps, worn at the waist by men and women, from which the small items were suspended. Although not always connected with sewing, they were used for keeping such sewing accessories as thimbles, scissors, and *étuis* about the person. Examples still complete with original attachments are desirable; however, even the detachable individual items may be collectible in their own right.

◀ **ARTS AND CRAFTS**
The inset cabochon stones and hand-hammered finish on the collar of this pincushion are highly characteristic of the Arts and Crafts style of the late 19th and early 20thC. Made in 1905 by the firm of Deakin & Francis, this example features a hinged top, which opens to reveal a silk-lined interior where trinkets or jewelry could be stored. It may also have been used as a cushion for hatpins or hairpins. $480–560

▶ **PINCUSHION PRODUCTION**
The bases of most antique pincushions were made from two pieces of sheet silver that were assembled together and "loaded" for stability with pitch, wood or plaster of Paris. A velvet cover, as on this "swan" (1902) was typical. Companies specializing in the production of pincushions in the early 20thC include Adie & Lovekin and Chrisford & Norris, both of Birmingham. $160–240

◀ **NOVELTY PINCUSHIONS**
Pincushions were produced in great numbers during the Edwardian period. They were often made in animal and bird forms, including "lambs", "parrots", "camels", "swans", and "pigs", as shown here (1906). Unusual "animals", such as "alligators", are especially sought after by collectors. $320–480

COLLECTING

Other sewing
tools to be found
in antiques shops
and at fairs and
auctions include:
- bodkins
- bodkin cases
- crochet hooks
- buttonhooks
- needlecases
- *nécessaires*
- shears
- shuttles
- stilettos (used
for piercing cloth)
- tatting sets

▶ RIBBON THREADERS

Made in the USA in
the late 19thC, these
"fish" in graduated
sizes are ribbon
threaders, designed to
hold different widths of
ribbon through the slits
in their "tails". Made
from flat strips of silver
stamped with "fish
scales", they are
charming and highly
decorative. The value
of items in sets is
increased if, as here,
the set is complete.
$400–480

◀ HEMMING GAUGES

Hemming gauges,
used as guides
for measuring the
hems of trousers or
skirts, were sometimes
produced in silver.
This late 19thC
American example,
which is one of a pair,
features decorative
heart-shaped terminals,
with measurements
marked in inches and
a sliding cursor for
adjusting the length
of the hem. Decorative
and functional, they
are very collectible.
$160–240
(for the pair)

CHÂTELAINES

Châtelaines are ornamental clasps worn on a
belt or girdle during the day, from which
several small objects for household use were
hung on short chains. The earliest English
examples date from the 17thC and were
usually intended to hold a seal and watch.
It later became the fashion to use them for
holding all sorts of objects, from scissors,
keys, and pomanders to tape measures,
thimbles, and bodkin cases.

◀ DECORATIVE CHÂTELAINES

The daintiness and
decorative design of
this paste-set *châtelaine*
with spring clasps
(*c.*1760) indicate that it
was probably made for
a lady. Most likely of
German or Austrian
origin, it is still
complete with an
original key (shown),
which adds to its value.
An original case would
also increase the price.
$1,200–2,400

POMANDERS & VINAIGRETTES

In their simplest form pomanders, which were believed to protect the wearer against the plague, were merely oranges stuffed with cloves and held in the hands or silver cases containing balls of solid scent or spices and worn as pendants from chains or *châtelaines*. However, even from an early date elaborate novelty-shaped pomanders were also made. Vinaigrettes, which were inspired by pomanders and made from the late 18th until the late 19thC, are tiny hinged boxes designed to hold sponges that were soaked in perfume, aromatic salts, or vinegar and concealed under pierced hinged silver grilles; they were carried in pockets and sniffed to combat fainting fits or unpleasant smells caused by primitive sewage and water systems. Early vinaigrettes were very small, with simple grilles and engraved tops; by the 1830s they were generally larger, with more elaborate decoration and fancier grilles.

WHY THE NAME "POMANDER"?

The word "pomander" is derived from *pomme d'ambre* (French for "apple of amber"), which is a strong-smelling secretion of the sperm whale that is widely used in the production of perfume.

▶ POMANDERS

Some pomanders contained up to 16 compartments, each for a different scented oil or spice. This German example (*c.*1700) has three separate sections for solid perfume. Both men and women in the 16th and 17thC wore memento mori jewelry as a reminder of the transience of life; the skull shape makes this item very desirable. $2,400–2,880

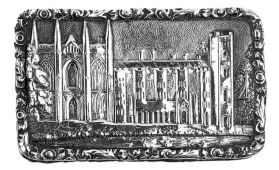

◀ "CASTLE-TOPS"

Among the most sought-after vinaigrettes are those known as "castle-tops", which feature decoration of famous landmarks and were possibly sold to travellers as souvenirs. This example (1845) shows Newstead Abbey. $1,600–2,400

▶ NOVELTY FORMS

The Victorian fancy for novelties found expression in an unlimited variety of vinaigrettes produced in the mid-19thC, including examples in the shapes of shells, fish, watches, crowns, flowers, and purses. Book-shaped vinaigrettes, as seen here (1853), often celebrated popular authors, including Sir Walter Scott or Lord Byron, with the author's name engraved on the spine. Others were made to commemorate historical events such as Admiral Nelson's victory at Trafalgar in 1805 or the Great Exhibition of 1851. $480–640

▼ GRILLES

Vinaigrettes are often collected exclusively for the decorative patterns found on their grilles, as on this example (1810) by Matthew Linwood. Early 19thC versions were pierced with simple geometric patterns or foliate scrolls; later 19thC grilles were more elaborate. Those in fanciful designs – hunt or battle scenes, military trophies, animals, birds, musical instruments, or filigree work – are the most valuable. $800–960

◀ DECORATION

Decoration on late 19thC vinaigrettes is mostly more elaborate than on early 19thC examples. Engine-turned scrollwork and floral motifs, as featured on this example of 1860, were popular, as was the fashion of engraving vinaigrettes with the owner's initials or a crest. The interiors of vinaigrettes were always gilded to protect the silver from corrosion caused by the aromatic perfume oil. Sometimes attempts (usually self-evident) are made to fashion a pill or snuff box from a vinaigrette by removing the grille. $160–320

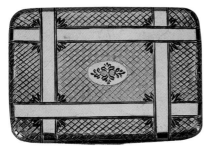

IMPORTANT MAKERS

Makers who are especially celebrated for their vinaigrettes include:

London
● Sampson Mordan & Co.

Birmingham
● Nathaniel Mills (particularly famed for "castle-top" vinaigrettes)
● Thomas Shaw
● Joseph Taylor

▼ SIZE

This novelty vinaigrette (c.1820) carved from agate has been mounted with a silver-gilt ram's head that hinges open to reveal a tiny perfume-soaked sponge hidden beneath the grille. Most vinaigrettes are fairly small, so that it was easy to keep them about the person, and this example is tiny (1⅜in/4cm). Ladies usually kept their vinaigrettes close to hand, either slipped into a glove or carried inside a muff or dainty beaded purse. $800–1,120

CARD CASES

Although the practice of presenting calling cards was widespread in polite society throughout the 18thC, it was not until the 1820s that cases were made specifically for them. The use of calling cards was grounded in subtle social etiquette, and card cases were typically made of such valuable materials as silver and intricately decorated to reflect the status of the owner. Most early card cases were oblong and made of silver gilt, usually with pierced or filigree decoration on both sides and sharply angled corners to fit the shape of the cards. As with snuff boxes and cigarette cases, the main center of manufacture in Britain was Birmingham. The peak period for production was between 1840 and 1860, which coincided with the burgeoning fashion for travel by rail. Many card cases found today feature architectural scenes and views of British landmarks. Known as "castle-tops" and popularly made as souvenirs, card cases of this type are very collectible.

▲ "CASTLE-TOPS"

The most popular card cases were those die-stamped with scenes of well-known monuments, cathedrals, or stately homes and known as "castle-tops". Typical British landmarks featured on these cases include Windsor Castle, St Paul's Cathedral and Warwick Castle. The rarest examples – such as views of Buckingham Palace – are keenly sought after by collectors and command the highest prices. The earliest "castle-tops" featured a scene on both sides, whereas later ones usually had a scene on one side only. The central panel with a scenic view was separately stamped in relief from a steel die and inset into the body of the case, with a chased or engraved decorative border surrounding it. Although the quality of card cases generally remains constant, those few with noticeably more detail or hand finishing are especially sought after. Snuff boxes were also made as "castle-tops", as from the 1830s were vinaigrettes. Certain makers, such as the Birmingham silversmith Nathaniel Mills, specialized in the production of "castle-tops". $1,120–4,800 (each – depending on the view)

NATHANIEL MILLS

The Birmingham maker Nathaniel Mills entered his first mark in 1825. He is especially celebrated for his production of "castle-top" card cases and vinaigrettes (see pp.154–5), and the majority of his production dates to the third quarter of the 19thC. One of his marks is shown below.

▶ EXOTIC MATERIALS

In the last quarter of the 19thC many card cases were made in the Far East to satisfy the prevailing European taste for Oriental wares. Typically made from silver combined with such exotic materials as ivory, tortoiseshell, mother-of-pearl, and lacquer, and lined with ivory or silk, these cases were produced in China, generally as souvenirs for gentlemen conducting business in Shanghai or Canton. On this example (*c.*1880) the figures have been stamped out from thin sheet silver and applied to the tortoiseshell. Because the layer of tortoiseshell is wafer-thin, it is very delicate and tends to deteriorate over time. The value of a card case will be drastically reduced if the case is in poor condition, so avoid dented examples (difficult to repair) and those with weak or damaged hinges. $320–400

◀ JAPANESE INFLUENCE

Following the invasion of Japanese territorial waters by the US Navy in 1853, which forced Japan to accept diplomatic relations and re-establish trade with the West, all things Oriental were in vogue. Such card cases as this ivory example (*c.*1880) decorated with *shibayama* work became popular. Although these cases are highly sought after today, this example is in poor condition, which reduces its value. $480–800

▶ ELABORATE INTERIORS

This card case, produced in 1871 by the London maker W. Thornhill, features a concertina-style interior made of silk-covered cardboard and is a good example of the inventive interiors found in some card cases. This case is elaborately decorated with engine-turned foliage and has a vacant cartouche. Some cases, intended to hold money or stamps, featured a clip for security. $160–480

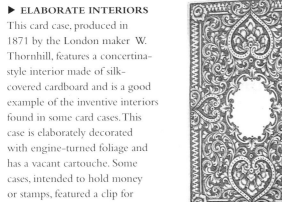

NURSERY WARE

Many fine silver articles for the nursery have survived in good condition, owing to a large degree because they were traditionally given as christening presents, and consequently treasured and protected. Novelty items such as rattles, designed to be sucked by teething babies, have been produced in silver since the Middle Ages; made from the mid-18thC in large numbers, in silver, silver gilt, and gold, they are quirky and relatively inexpensive collectibles. Most rattles feature a coral handle or teether, which was not only durable but also originally believed to ward off evil spirits. Among the traditional types of gift made to commemorate the christening of a child and presented to the parents to keep for the child, were boxed sets, which variously included child-size knives, forks, spoons, mugs, and bowls; apostle spoons, with finials in the form of the apostles; cups and mugs decorated with childhood themes; and silver picture frames, used for displaying babies' photographs.

◀ FITTED CHRISTENING BOWL-AND-SPOON SETS
Silver bowls and spoons fitted in a silk-lined case, as in this example (1912), were often given as gifts to commemorate the christening of a baby. The bowls were frequently engraved with scenes depicting familar nursery rhymes, Mother Goose stories, or other themes from childhood. Examples in their original boxes and in good condition can still be purchased for relatively modest sums and are very good value. $400–560

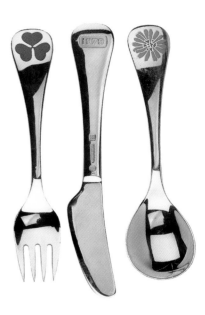

▶ RATTLES
This typical Victorian rattle (1865) consists of a whistle, bells, and a coral teething stick for a baby to chew, which in some versions was made of ivory. The condition of rattles is important, so look carefully for loose or damaged bells or coral, or replacements. A rare early example, or one made by a known silversmith such as Hester Bateman, would fetch a very high price. $480–640

▲ CUTLERY SETS
This beautifully made knife, fork and spoon set has been decorated at the top of the stems with colorful enameling. This technique is characteristic of Scandinavian design and was used to produce a variety of decorative patterns, often incorporating the birthday or name of the child. Makers such as the firm of Georg Jensen produced such children's utensil sets in a wide variety of styles from the 1950s. $95–160

ENGRAVING

Engraved initials or inscriptions lower the value of a piece unless they were added for important historical purposes. If engraving has been removed, check the quality of the silver by pressing it gently, as it may be thin and vulnerable to damage.

▲ FAMOUS MAKERS

Christening bowl-and-spoon sets by well-known makers such as Tiffany & Co. or the Gorham Manufacturing Co. are especially desirable. Some sets were also made with matching saucers, such as this fine late 19thC silver-gilt set by Tiffany, which shows a pond scene with decoration of leaping "frogs" and "lily pads", with the bowl of the saucer as the "pond". Examples such as this are especially sought after in the USA. $960–1,600

▶ NURSERY MUGS

Mugs have also traditionally been given as christening presents, sometimes in sets with other nursery ware, and were made in large quantities from 1850 to 1900. This parcel-gilded example (1940s) has been charmingly decorated with the letters of the alphabet, and as a mug in good condition featuring eye-catching bold colors it is very desirable. $320–480

APOSTLE SPOONS

Apostle spoons were made in England from the mid-15thC, although the fashion for them had waned by the mid-17thC. Produced in vast numbers, they are so-called because the cast finials portray the twelve apostles, each identified by the emblem carried in his right hand. Apostle spoons were originally made in sets of 12 or 13 (including Christ), but complete sets are extremely rare. Apostle spoons were often given as christening presents to boys, with the child receiving the spoon bearing the apostle after whom he was named. Sometimes dedications or initials and dates are found engraved on the backs of the faceted stems. Apostle spoons tend to command high prices today; however, beware of fakes made by shaping the bowls of tablespoons into the fig shape typical of the bowls of apostle spoons and attaching a reproduction apostle finial. $3,200–8,000+

MISCELLANEOUS I

The variety of small novelty objects produced from silver presents collectors with an exceptionally rich choice. Small items for personal use, such as boxes, buckles, posy holders, letter openers, gentlemen's *étuis,* and sovereign holders, are but a few examples of the enormous assortment of reasonably priced collectibles on the market today. From the late 18thC the city of Birmingham in Britain held pride of place as the premier center for the production of small silver articles and trinkets for everyday use. When the mechanized manufacture of silver was developed in the 19thC, these popular items were produced in prodigious numbers, and they continue to offer limitless opportunities for assembling an imaginative collection for a relatively modest sum.

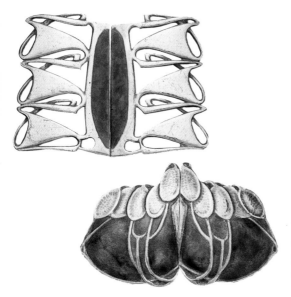

◀ BUCKLES

The fashion for wearing buckles instead of shoelaces was taken up in England in the 17thC, and in the 18thC they were commonly used to anchor neckbands and sashes as well as to fasten shoes and knee breeches. In the late 19th and early 20thC intricate Art Nouveau buckles, with trailing scrolls, stylized boat patterns, and lily pads as shown (both *c.*1900), and often featuring colored enameling, provided decorative embellishment to ladies' belts, threaded onto a fabric strap. Both parts of the buckle should be hallmarked. Buckles produced by such well-known makers as Tiffany & Co., Liberty & Co. and Omar Ramsden are highly sought after and, if signed, should fetch a handsome premium. $480–640 (each)

▶ POSY HOLDERS

Posy holders, such as this example (1870) stamped from thin sheet silver and decorated with an abundance of lily flowers, were very fashionable in the mid-19thC. They were designed for holding nosegays or single flowers and attached to the bodice of a dress. A silver funnel containing a moistened sponge holds the posy stem, which is secured by a small pin or spike. Some posy holders are designed to be worn as brooches, while examples such as this one have a finger ring attached to a small chain, which could be used when it was carried in the hand. If the ball finial is pulled, the spring-loaded handle flicks into a three-legged stand to make a practical posy vase. $480–640

◀ GENTLEMEN'S ETUIS

This late 18thC English *étui* has a wooden interior designed to contain a tiny steel fork, knife and ear pick, a pair of folding steel scissors with silver handles, and a silver spoon. Often called "gentlemen's *étuis*", such cases were used by men when traveling, typically hung from *châtelaines*. 1,280–1,440

BEWARE

Any intricate decoration is prone to damage, which will lower the value.

▶ BOOKS MOUNTED IN SILVER

Leather books fitted with silver covers, as on this modern example (1995), are popular. Books or bibles with silver clasps of 17th and 18thC Dutch or German origin are rare and valuable, but many 19thC silver-mounted books are extremely affordable. Check the condition, as the silver is fairly fragile. $30–50

◀ SOVEREIGN HOLDERS

This small silver case (1892), designed in the form of a pocket watch, has been fitted inside with a spring-loaded compartment to hold four or five gold sovereign coins. The sovereign holder kept pocket money handy when it was attached to a chain or *châtelaine* by means of the small swivel ring that can be seen on top. $160–190

◀ ART NOUVEAU

In the late 19thC and early 20thC many timepieces (clocks that do not strike) such as this one (*c.*1900) were made in the Art Nouveau style. Enamel decoration adds value, as does the name of a top maker: for example, Liberty & Co. or Omar Ramsden. $800–1,120

OMAR RAMSDEN

Omar Ramsden (1873–1939) was one of the leading turn of the century metalsmiths. Wares are stamped or incised as shown (literally meaning "Omar Ramsden made me").

OMAR RAMSDEN ME FECIT

MISCELLANEOUS II

Although such items as parasols, toothbrush sets, tongue-scrapers, and lamps are essentially practical, the versions featured here have been transformed into desirable collectibles through the imaginations of highly skilled silversmiths. Some items such as freedom boxes – presented when a person was granted the freedom of a city in recognition of his or her service to the public – may be of note not only for their fine workmanship but also for their historical interest. Other items, such as butt markers, used to determine where each member of a grouse-shooting party should stand, may appeal, for example, to sports fans or those interested in social history. To avoid favoritism or an unseemly scramble for the best shooting spot, pegs, or butts, were drawn from a case to decide each participant's place in the line formed to drive the grouse across the moor.

◀ BUTT MARKERS
This valuable butt marker – also known as a butt selector – in the form of a small vesta case has a gilded interior and contains small pegs marked with numbers in the form of shotgun cartridges. Butt markers were most popular between the 1880s and the first decade of the 20thC and were made in vast numbers by the celebrated Dee family of silversmiths. $1,600–2,400

▶ PARASOLS
Silk parasols with ivory handles fitted with richly decorated silver mounts were produced in large numbers in the 19thC for the hot climates of the colonial settlements in India and the Far East. Local silversmiths were commonly employed to fashion the silver mounts for walking canes, swagger sticks, riding crops, and parasols, which are rarely hallmarked. Not very practical for use today, a parasol in good condition such as this example (c.1900) can be relatively affordable. $80–160

▶ FREEDOM BOXES
Engraved on one side with the arms of a city and on the other with a dedication, a freedom box was presented when a person was granted the freedom of a city. Most were fairly small – approximately 2¾in (7cm) in diameter – and made in silver; however, some fine examples were also made in gold. It is rare to find freedom boxes complete with the original papers granting the freedom of a city, but if the latter are present they will add to the value. Provincial examples, particularly Irish ones, are very collectible. $3,200–4,000

CONDITION CHECKLIST
● On items with delicate decoration, check for thin, worn, or cracked silver. Filigree decoration and ornamentation in high relief are particularly prone to damage.
● Check handles or hinges, which are easy to damage.
● Look for signs of repair around handles, feet, or rims.
● Check the surface for signs of excessive polishing or erasure.

◀ TOOTHPOWDER BOX AND TOOTHBRUSH

This portable silver box (1791) has a double-hinged cover opening and two compartments, designed to accommodate both coarse and finely milled toothpowders. Similar sets often also include a tongue-scraper. This hallmarked toothbrush set in its original tooled leather box is rare and desirable. $1,280–1,600

▶ TONGUE-SCRAPERS

Made in silver and old Sheffield plate and often unmarked, tongue-scrapers such as this example (1790) by John Death were popular during the reign of George III (1760–1820). In this design the flexible U-shape is held by the twisted ends and drawn across the tongue to eliminate the pink stain caused by drinking red wine. Another variation on the tongue-scraper is one in the form of a small rake. An early silver example is a great rarity and would be worth several thousand pounds. Tongue-scrapers are sometimes found in toothbrush box sets (*see* above). $480–640

◀ LAMPS

First produced in old Sheffield plate in the late 18thC, portable lamps were commonly used by travelers or to enable late-night reading by industrious students. This late Victorian silver lamp (1880s) has a gilded interior to spread the light efficiently, a telescopic tubular stand that pushes into the body and a flap that folds over to protect the glass. The top hinges open to make lighting a candle easy, and the concertina back allows the smoke to escape. A trio of crescent-shaped feet provide the stand with stability. Fairly rare in silver, these lamps are subject to damage and wear from frequent use. $2,400–3,200

FAKES

- Marks that have soft outlines may be fake.
- Breathing on the surface will reveal the solder around marks that have been transposed.
- Metal may be thin where armorials have been removed, which will lower the value.

PART 5

INFORMATION

ABOVE VALUABLE SOURCES OF INFORMATION ON
COLLECTING ANTIQUES.

LEFT A GRAND DISPLAY OF DINING SILVER.

WHERE TO BUY & SEE

WHERE TO BUY

Silver can be purchased through many sources, including auction houses, antiques dealers, markets, fairs, and car-boot sales. Below is just a selection of useful names and addresses to start you off.

MAJOR AUCTION HOUSES (USA)

Christie's
502 Park Avenue
New York
NY 10022

Christie's East
219 East 67th Street
New York
NY 10021

Sotheby's
1334 York Avenue
New York
NY 10021

Sotheby's
215 West Ohio Street
Chicago
IL 60610

Butterfield & Butterfield
220 San Bruno Avenue
San Francisco
CA 94103

Skinner Inc.
357 Main Street
Boston
MA 01740

MAJOR AUCTION HOUSES (UK)

Christie's South Kensington
85 Old Brompton Road
South Kensington
London SW7

Dreweatt & Neate
Donnington Priory
Donnington
Newbury

Lots Road Auction Galleries
71 Lots Road
Chelsea
London SW10

Phillips
101 New Bond Street
London W1

Sotheby's
34–35 New Bond Street
London W1

Sotheby's Sussex
Summers Place
Billingshurst
West Sussex

MAJOR ANTIQUES FAIRS (USA)

Baltimore Museum Antiques Show
Baltimore Museum
of Art
10 Art Museum Drive
Baltimore
MD 21218

Connecticut Spring Antiques Show
State Armory
Hartford CT

Ellis Memorial Hospital Show
The Cyclorama
539 Tremont Street
Boston MA

Fall Show at the Armory
Seventh Regiment
Armory
67th and Park Avenue
New York
NY 10021

Heart of Country Antiques Show
Opryland Hotel
2800 Opryland Drive
Nashville
TN 37214

International Fine Art and Antique Dealers Show
Seventh Regiment
Armory
67th Street and Park
Avenue
New York
NY 10021

Mid-Week Manchester Antiques Show
Sheraton Tara
Wayfarer Inn
Bedford
NH

New Hampshire Antique Dealers Association Show
Center of New
Hampshire
Holiday Inn
700 Elm Street
Manchester
NH 03101

New York Winter Antiques Show
Seventh Regiment
Armory
67th Street and Park
Avenue
New York
NY 10021

Philadelphia Antiques Show
103rd Engineers Armory
33rd and Market Streets
Phildelphia
PA 19104

Washington Antiques Show
Omni Shorham Hotel
2500 Calvert Street NW
Washington DC

Riverside Antiques Show
New Hampshire
State Armory
Canal Street
Manchester
NH 03101

San Francisco Fall Antiques Show
Fort Mason Center
Festival Pavilion
San Francisco
CA 94123

WHERE TO SEE

Visiting major collections in museums and houses open to the public is an invaluable way to learn more about silver. Listed below are some places to visit with important silver collections in the USA.

Albany Institute of History & Art
125 Washington Avenue
Albany
NY 12210

Bayou Bend Connection Museum of Fine Arts
PO Box 6826
Houston
Texas 77006–1243

The Brooklyn Museum
200 Eastern Parkway
Brooklyn
NY 11238–6052

The Cleveland Museum of Art
11150 East Boulevard
Cleveland
OH 44106

Colonial Williamsburg
PO Box 1776
Williamsburg
VA 23187–1776

Currier Gallery of Art
201 Myrtle Way
Manchester
NH 03104

**The Detroit
Institute of Arts**
5200 Woodward Avenue
Detroit
MI 48202

**William Hayes Fogg
Art Museum**
Harvard University
32 Quiney Street
Cambridge
MA 02138

Henry Ford Museum
20900 Oakwood
Boulevard
Dearborn
MI 48124

**The Henry Francis
du Pont Winterthur
Museum**
Route 52
Winterthur
Delaware
DE 19735

**The Metropolitan
Museum of Art**
100 Fifth Avenue
New York
NY 19928–0198

**The Minneapolis
Institute of Arts**
2400 Third Avenue South
Minneapolis
MN 055404

**Museum of the City
of New York**
1220 Fifth Avenue
New York
NY 10029

Museum of Fine Arts
465 Huntington Avenue
Boston
MA 02115–5519

**The New York
Historical Society**
2 W. 77th Street
Central Park West
New York
NY 10024

**Philadelphia
Museum of Art**
Pennsylvania
PO Box 7646
Philadelphia
PA 19130

**Museum of Art
Rhode Island
School of Design**
224 Benefit Street
Providence
Rhode Island
RI 02903–2723

**Smithsonian
Institution**
900 Jefferson Drive SW
Room 2410
MRC 421
Washington DC 20560

**Sterling &
Francine Clark
Art Institute**
PO Box 8
Williamstown
MA 01276

**Virginia Museum
of Fine Arts**
2800 Grove Avenue
Richmond
VA 23221–2472

**Wadsworth
Athenaeum**
600 Main Street
Hartford
Connecticut
CT 06103–2990

**Worcester Art
Museum**
55 Salisbury Street
Worcester
MA 01609–3196

**Yale University
Art Gallery**
PO Box 208271
New Haven
Connecticut
CT 06520–8271

**ANTIQUES
ASSOCIATIONS**
The following
trade associations offer
helpful information on
annual antiques fairs,
specialist dealers,
valuations, and
insurance.

**National Art &
Antiques Dealers'
Association
(NAADA)**
12 East 56th Street
New York
NY 10022

**Art and Antique
Dealers League
of America
(AADLA)**
353 East 78th Street
New York
NY 10021

**Professional Art
Dealers Association
of Canada**
296 Richmond Street
West
Toronto
Ontario
M5V 1X2

**The Association
of Art and
Antique Dealers
(LAPADA)**
535 King's Road
London SW10

**British Antique
Dealers' Association
(BADA)**
20 Rutland Gate
London SW7

SOCIETIES & CLUBS
Much useful collecting
information can be
obtained through
specialist societies
and clubs. For a more
comprehensive list of
organizations specializing
in silver, consult *Antique
Collecting*, the journal of
the Antique Collectors'
Club (ACC).

**Antique
Collectors' Club**
5 Church Street
Woodbridge
Suffolk

**Goldsmith's
Company**
Foster Lane
London EC2

The Silver Society
22 Orlando Road
London SW4

**The Silver
Spoon Club of
Great Britain**
Glenleigh Park
Sticker
St Austell

**The Silver
Study Group**
PO Box 93
London NW4

**The Society of Caddy
Spoon Collectors**
PO Box No. 219
Winchester
Hants

Thimble Society
Grays Antique Market
58 Davies Street
London W1

Wine Label Circle
45 Shepherd's Hill
London N6

WHAT TO READ

MAGAZINES & PERIODICALS

Antique Collecting
The Antique Dealer and Collectors' Guide
Antiques Magazine
The Antiques Trade Gazette
The Silver Magazine

GENERAL BOOKS

Blair, Claude (General Editor), *The History of Silver*, 1987
Bly, John, *Miller's Antiques Checklist: Silver & Silver Plate Marks*, 1993
Clayton, Michael, *The Collector's Dictionary of Silver and Gold of Great Britain and North America*, 1985
Helliwell, Stephen, *Understanding Silver Plate*, 1996
Langford, Joel, *Silver: A Practical Guide to Collecting Silverware and Identifying Hallmarks*, 1994
Miller, Judith (General Editor), *Miller's Antiques Encyclopedia*, 1998
Newman, Harold, *An Illustrated Dictionary of Silverware*, 1987
Pickford, Ian, *Antique Silver*, 1998
Truman, Charles (General Editor), *Sotheby's Concise Encyclopedia of Silver*, 1993
Waldron, Peter, *The Price Guide to Antique Silver*, 1982
Wilson, John, *Miller's Antiques Checklist: Silver & Plate*, 1994

FURTHER READING

Banister, Judith, *An Introduction to Old English Silver*, 1965
Bennett, D., *Collecting Irish Silver*, 1984
Bradbury, Frederick, *Bradbury's Book of Hallmarks*, 1975
Brett, Vanessa, *Sotheby's Directory of Silver*, 1985
Brunner, Herbert, *Old Table Silver*, 1967

Crisp-Jones, K. (Editor), *The Silversmiths of Birmingham*, 1981
Culme, John, *The Directory of Gold and Silversmiths 1838–1914*, 1987
Culme, John, *Nineteenth Century Silver*, 1976
Darbyshire, Lydia, *Antique Silver*, 1994
Davis, Frank, *French Silver 1450–1825*, 1970
Fales, M.G., *Early American Silver*, 1970
Gill, M.A.V., *A Directory of Newcastle Goldsmiths*, 1976
Glanville, Philippa, *Silver in England*, 1987
Glanville, Philippa, *Silver in Tudor and Early Stuart England*, 1991
Glanville, Philippa (Editor), *Silver*, 1996
Grimwade, Arthur, *Rococo Silver 1727–1765*, 1974
Grimwade, Arthur, *London Goldsmiths 1697–1837, Their Marks and Lives*, 1976
Gruber, A., *Silverware*, 1985
Hartop, Christopher, *The Huguenot Legacy, English Silver 1680–1760*, 1996
Hayward, J.F., *Huguenot Silver in England 1688–1727*, 1959
Helliwell, Stephen, *Small Silver Tableware: The Connoisseur's Guide*, 1996
Hernmarck, C., *The Art of the European Silversmith 1430–1830*, 1977
Hughes, Graham, *Modern Silver Throughout the World*, 1967
Hughes, Graham, *Small Antique Silverware*, 1971
Hughes, Eleanor, *Silver for Collectors*, 1990
Jackson, Sir Charles James, *English Goldsmiths and Their Marks*, 1921 (reprinted 1964)

Jackson, Sir Charles James, *Jackson's Silver and Gold Marks of England, Scotland and Ireland*, 1989
Kent, T.A., *London Silver Spoonmakers 1500–1679*, 1981
Kovel, Ralph M. & Terry H., *American Silver, Pewter and Silver Plate*, 1961
Knowles, Eric, *Miller's Antiques Checklist: Victoriana*, 1991
Krekel-Aalberse, Annelies, *Art Nouveau and Art Deco Silver*, 1989
Luddington, John, *Starting to Collect Silver*, 1988
Norie, John, *Caddy Spoons*, 1988
Oman, Charles, *Caroline Silver 1625–1688*, 1970
Oman, Charles, *English Engraved Silver 1150–1900*, 1978
Oman, Charles, *English Domestic Silver*, 1967
Pearsall, Ronald, *A Connoisseur's Guide to Antique Silver*, 1997
Penzer, N.M., *Paul Storr*, 1954
Phillips, P., *Paul de Lamerie*, 1935
Pickford, Ian, *Silver Flatware 1660–1980*, 1983
Rainwater, Dorothy T., *Encyclopedia of American Silver Manufacturers*, 1986
Rowe, Robert, *Adam Silver*, 1965
Schroder, Timothy, *The Gilbert Collection of Gold and Silver*, 1988
Schroder, Timothy, *English Domestic Silver 1500–1900*, 1988
Snodin, M., *Silver Spoons*, 1982
Stancliffe, J., *Silver Bottle Tickets*, 1986
Taylor, Gerald, *Silver Through the Ages*, 1964
Waldron, Peter, *The Price Guide to Antique Silver*, 1982
Wardle, P., *Victorian Silver*, 1963
Wees, Beth Carver, *English, Irish and Scottish Silver at the Sterling and Francine Clark Institute*, 1998

GLOSSARY

Acanthus Classical ornament in the form of stylized leaf decoration based on the scalloped leaves of the acanthus plant.

Adam Style Neo-classical style, first introduced into Britain by the Scottish architect/designer Robert Adam, typified by Classical motifs such as palmettes and festoons.

Alloy Amalgam formed of two or more metals. In silver, the base metals added for strength.

Annealing Process for restoring the malleability of silver or other metals made brittle by hammering. The metal is heated until red hot and then immersed in cold water.

Anthemion Stylized ornament derived from Classical architecture based on the honeysuckle flower.

Applied work Wire, molding, or cast pieces made separately and soldered on to the main body of a piece, to ornament or strengthen it.

Argyll Vessel resembling a small coffeepot and designed for keeping gravy warm.

Armorial Engraved crest or coat-of-arms.

Assay Testing metal to establish its purity.

Baluster Bulbous pillar shape, commonly used for vases, jugs, and teapots, finials and the stems of some candlesticks and drinking vessels.

Bayonet fitting Method of attaching a cover to a body by means of two locking lugs that are slotted into a flange and rotated.

Beading Decorative border of tiny compact beads, either cast and applied or embossed.

Bright-cut decoration Type of engraving whereby the metal surface is cut creating facets that reflect the light.

Britannia metal Electroplated pewter used as a metal substitute for silver.

Britannia standard Higher standard of British silver used between 1697 and 1720; contains 95.8% pure silver.

Burnishing Method of polishing metals by rubbing the surface with a hard, smooth tool, such as agate, to create a luster.

Caddy spoon Spoon for taking a measure of tea from a caddy.

Candelabrum Candlestick with arms and nozzles for two or more candles.

Cartouche Decorative shield, normally engraved, embossed, or cast, and generally containing an inscription or coat-of-arms.

Caster Vessel with a pierced cover, for sprinkling salt, sugar, or ground pepper.

Casting Process for making metal objects or their components, whereby molten metal is poured into a mold and then soldered onto other parts.

Caudle cup Two-handled vessel, used for drinking gruel.

Chamberstick Utilitarian candlestick with a short stem and saucer-like base.

Charger Large circular or oval dish or plate, often richly decorated.

Chasing Method of decorating silver using hammers and punches to push metal into a relief pattern; metal is displaced not removed.

Chinoiserie European fashion for decorating silver with Oriental figures and scenes, including birds, pagodas, and lotus flowers, in vogue in the late 17thC and again in the mid-18thC.

Crest Heraldic device surmounting a coat-of-arms, used to denote ownership.

Cruet Frame for holding casters and bottles (for condiments).

Cut-card decoration Flat shapes of applied silver used as decoration and for reinforcement.

Die-stamping Method of pressing sheet silver between solid dies with complementary patterns to create or decorate an item.

Dish ring Used to protect the table surface from damage caused by hot plates.

Electroplating Method of using an electric current to coat one metal with another (usually silver over an alloy).

Engraving Decorative patterns cut into the silver surface using a sharp tool; metal is actually removed.

Epergne Centerpiece consisting of a central bowl and several small detachable bowls to display and serve fruit and sweetmeats.

Erasure Removal of an existing coat-of-arms on silver that is sometimes replaced by new arms.

Ewer Large jug with a lip that is often part of a set including a basin.

Faceted Decorative surface cut into sharp-edged planes in a criss-cross pattern to reflect the light.

Filigree Openwork silver or gold wire panels.

Finial Decorative turned knob.

Flat chasing Chasing on a flat silver surface, leaving an impression of the punched pattern on the back.

Flatware All flat and shallow tableware, such as plates and salvers, but more specifically applied to spoons and forks.

Fluting Pattern of concave grooves repeated in vertical, parallel lines.

Gadrooning Border composed of a succession of alternating lobes and flutes, usually curved.

Gauge Thickness of a metal sheet or the diameter of a wire.

Gilding Process of applying a gold finish to a silver or electroplated object.

Hallmarks Marks on silver that indicate it has been passed at assay. The term derives from the Goldsmiths' Hall, London, where the marks were struck.

Hollow ware Any hollow vessels, such as bowls and teapots.

Huguenot French Protestants who settled in England and The Netherlands following the Revocation of the Edict of Nantes in 1685, which denied them religious freedom. Many were skilled silversmiths, weavers and furniture makers, who introduced French styles into the decorative arts of England and Holland.

Ingot Piece of cast metal obtained from a mold in a form suitable for storage.

Knop Decorative knob on lids, or the bulbous molding, usually placed at the mid-point of the stem of a cup or candlestick.

Liner Inner sleeve of a vessel, made of silver, plate, or glass.

Loading System for strengthening and stabilizing hollow objects, such as candlesticks or candelabra, whereby an iron rod is secured inside the body using pitch or plaster of Paris.

Matting Non-shiny texture produced by punching small dots or circles closely over the surface, commonly found contrasting with highly burnished surfaces.

Monteith Cooler for wine glasses, resembling a punchbowl, but with a notched rim to suspend the glasses over iced water.

Mote spoon Small spoon with a pierced bowl used to skim tea leaves, with a spike at the end of the stem to unblock the spout of the teapot.

Molding Silver decoration cast in a mold.

Nickel Any of various white alloys of copper, zinc, and nickel used in electroplating as a base for coating with silver.

Niello Compound of silver, lead, copper, and sulphur applied to metal and fired to create a shimmering black surface.

Nozzle On a candlestick, the detachable top in which the candle is placed.

Openwork Pierced decoration.

Parcel gilt Silver partially covered with gold.

Patina Fine, natural sheen of age on the surface of silver.

Piercing Intricate cut decoration, created by using a sharp chisel or fretsaw, and then punches.

Plate Originally applied to gold and silver domestic wares, this term now tends to refer to articles made of base metal and covered with silver, either by

fusion, such as Sheffield plate, or by electroplating.

Planish Initial stage in finishing the surface of plate before polishing, to remove the hammer marks which occur during raising, by using a special flat-headed hammer.

Plinth Square base at the bottom of a candlestick column.

Porringer Two-handled dish, sometimes with a lid, originally used to hold porridge or gruel.

Raising Process by which a piece of hollow ware is hammered into shape, using annealed silver.

Rat's tail Short ridge of silver applied to the back of spoon bowls to reinforce the joint at the handle.

Reeding Decorative molding composed of narrow parallel convex threadlike forms, usually confined to borders.

Repoussé Term for embossing. Relief decoration on metal is made by hammering from the reverse so that the decoration projects, then is finished from the front by chasing.

Rolled edge Edges of Sheffield plate or fused-plate articles were rolled to conceal the copper centre, which would otherwise be visible.

Salver Flat dish, sometimes footed, for serving food or drink; similar to a tray but with no handles and often with a molded border and decorated with an engraved coat-of-arms.

Sconce Candle socket of a candlestick. Also, a plate or bracket on the wall to which candle-holders could be attached.

Scratchweight Note made of the weight of a silver article at assay, usually hand engraved lightly on the base or reverse; any change from the original weight may indicate that the piece has been altered or overly polished; with silver in sets, such as plates, the number of the individual piece was often also inscribed on the base, which may help with building up a complete set.

Scroll Curved decoration, particularly used for handles.

Shagreen Untanned leather, originally the skin of the shagri, a Turkish wild ass; now used to refer to any granulated leather.

Sheet Sheet silver and sheet metal describe the panels of silver and plate used primarily in the manufacture of candlesticks.

Sheffield plate Silver substitute used from *c.*1740, made by binding and fusing together sterling silver and copper.

Silver gilt Solid silver covered with a thin layer of gold.

Snuffer Scissor-like implement for trimming and collecting wicks.

Solder Usually of lead, applied to repair cracks and holes.

Spoonmaker Term used to describe a maker of flatware.

Standard Required amount of pure silver in an alloy.

Sterling silver British term for silver that is at least 92.5% pure.

Stirrup cup Cup used for drinking prior to making a journey or going hunting. Usually shaped as the head of an animal.

Swag Suspended festoon of foliage, flowers, fruit, or drapery.

Tankard Mug with a hinged cover, usually for beer.

Taperstick Small candlestick for holding a taper (thin candle) for lighting pipes and melting wax.

Tazza Wide shallow bowl on a stemmed foot.

Tumbler cup Round-bottomed drinking vessel.

Tureen Large bowl on a foot for serving soup.

Vesta box Ornate case for carrying matches.

Vinaigrette Small silver box with an inner pierced lid to hold a sponge soaked in a vinegar.

Waiter Small salver, less than 6in (15cm) in diameter.

White metal Hard alloy of copper and zinc used as a base in electroplating.

INDEX

ACKNOWLEDGMENTS

The publishers would like to thank the following dealers, collectors, and auction houses for supplying pictures for use in this book or for allowing their pieces to be photographed. Special thanks to the Fay Lucas Gallery and the London Silver Vaults. The author would like to thank Liz Stubbs (Commissioning Editor) for her invaluable guidance and generous support, Clare Peel (Editor) for her enthusiasm, constant good spirits, and skilful editing, Alexis Butcher for his buoyant good humor, and Edward Bace for his never-ending encouragement.

Front jacket cl, c, cr, b OPG/AJP/CSK, **tl** CI, **tc** S, **tr** P; **front jacket flap** OPG/AJP/FL; **back jacket** OPG/AJP/FL; **back jacket flap** OPG/AJP/CSK
2 tl OPG/AJP/CSK, **tcl** OPG/AJP/CSK, **tcr** S, **tr** OPG/AJP/CSK, **cl** S, **c** OPG/AJP/CSK, **bl** CI, **br** OPG/IB/S; **3 tl** CI, **tr** CI, **c** CI/CSK, **bl** OPG/AJP/IB/S, **br** S; **8 tl** CI, **tr** S, **bl** CI, **br** CI; **9 tl** OPG/AJP/CSK, **tr** OPG/AJP/FL, **bl** OPG/AJP/FL, **br** OPG/AJP/NL; **10** OPG/AJP/CSK; **11** OPG/AJP/CSK; **12** OPG/AJP/CSK; **13 t** OPG/AJP/CSK, **b** CI; **14** OPG/AJP/PR; **15** OPG/AJP/CSK; **16** OPG/AJP/CSK; **17** OPG/AJP/CSK; **18** OPG/AJP/FL; **19** OPG/AJP/CSK; **20** OPG/AJP/IF; **21** OPG/AJP/RF; **22** photograph©NEC, Birmingham; **23** P; **24** OPG/AJP; **25** OPG/AJP; **26** AB; **27** OPG/AJP/CSK; **28** CNY; **29 tl** OPG/HJ, **tr** OPG/HJ, **b** OPG/AJP/CSK; **30** OPG/AJP; **31 t** OPG/AJP/CSK, **b** OPG/AJP/CSK; **32** OPG/JME; **33** AB; **34** SNY; **35** OPG/AJP/CSK; **36** OPG/AJP/CSK; **37** CI; **38 l** OPG/AJP/CSK, **tr** OPG/AJP/CSK, **b** OPG/AJP/CSK; **39 t** OPG/AJP/CSK, **c** CI, **bl** OPG/AJP/CSK; **40 l** OPG/AJP/CSK, **r** OPG/AJP/CSK; **41 l** OPG/AJP/CSK, **r** OPG/AJP/CSK; **42 tl** OPG/AJP/FL, **tr** OPG/AJP/CSK, **bl** OPG/AJP/FL, **br** OPG/AJP/CSK; **43 tl** OPG/AJP/CSK, **tr** OPG/AJP/CSK, **cl** OPG/AJP/CSK, **ct** OPG/AJP/CSK, **cb** OPG/AJP/CSK, **b** P; **44 t** OPG/AJP/FL, **cl** P, **c** OPG/AJP/FL, **cr** OPG/AJP/CSK, **bc** OPG/AJP/CSK, **br** OPG/AJP/CSK; **45 tl** OPG/AJP/CSK, **c** OPG/AJP/CSK, **bl** OPG/AJP/CSK, **r** OPG/AJP/CSK; **46 l** OPG/AJP/CSK, **r** OPG/AJP/CSK, **ct** OPG/AJP/CSK, **cb** OPG/AJP; **47 l** OPG/AJP/CSK, **tr** JN/CNY, **bl** JN/CNY; **48** OPG/AJP/CSK, **l** OPG/AJP/CSK, **tr** OPG/AJP/CSK, **c** OPG/AJP/CSK, **br** OPG/AJP/CSK; **49 tl** PG/AJP/CSK, **tr** OPG/AJP/CSK, **bl** OPG/AJP/CSK, **br** OPG/AJP/CSK; **50** P; **51** OPG/CSK; **52** SNY/1998 Sotheby's, Inc.; **53 t** S, **b** S; **54 t** OPG/IB, **b** S; **55 t** S, **c** CI, **b** S; **56** CI; **57 t** PC/B/BAL, **c** P, **b** OPG/AJP/FL; **58 l** OPG/AJP/FL, **c** OPG/AJP/FL, **r** OPG/AJP/CSK; **59 tl** CI, **tr** CI, **b** OPG/AJP/CSK; **60 t** S, **b** CI; **61 t** OPG/AJP/CSK, **bl** OPG/IB, **br** OPG/AJP/CSK; **62 t** CI, **bl** OPG/AJP/CSK, **br** SNY/1998 Sotheby's, Inc; **63 t** SNY/1998 Sotheby's, Inc., **c** P, **b** OPG/SC/NH; **64 t** OPG/AJP/CSK, **b** OPG/AJP/CSK; **65 tl** CI, **tr** CI, **bl** OPG/AJP/CSK, **br** CI; **66 tl** CI, **c** OPG/AJP/CSK, **bl** CI; **67 t** OPG/AJP/CSK, **cl** CI, **b** OPG/AJP/CSK; **68 t** CI, **c** CI, **b** OPG/AJP/CSK; **69 tl** JN/CNY, **r** S, **c** OPG/AJP/FL, **b** OPG/AJP/CSK; **70 t** CI, **b** CI; **71 tl** CI, **cl** P, **cr** CI, **b** CI; **72 t** OPG/IB/S, **c** CI, **b** CI; **73 t** OPG/AJP/CSK, **bl** OPG/IB, **br**

OPG/IB; **74 t** CI, **c** OPG/AJP/CSK, **b** CI; **75 t** S, **c** CI, **b** OPG/AJP/FL; **76 ct** S, **br** S; **77 t** OPG/AJP/CSK, **c** OPG/AJP/CSK, **b** OPG/AJP/CSK; **78 t** OPG/AJP/CSK, **b** CI; **79 t** OPG/AJP/FL, **c** OPG/AJP/CSK, **b** OPG/AJP/CSK; **80 t** OPG/IB, **b** OPG/AJP/CSK; **81 t** CI, **c** OPG/AJP/CSK, **b** OPG/AJP/CSK; **82 t** CI, **c** CI, **b** OPG/AJP/CSK; **83 t** OPG/AJP/CSK, **cl** OPG/AJP/FL, **cr** OPG/AJP/FL, **b** OPG/AJP/FL; **84 t** CI, **b** CI; **85 t** OPG/AJP/CSK, **c** CI, **bl** OPG/SC/NH, **br** OPG/AJP/CSK; **86 t** S, **b** CI; **87 t** OPG/AJP/CSK, **cl** P, **r** OPG/AJP/FL, **b** OPG/AJP/FL; **88 l** OPG/AJP/CSK, **c** OPG/AJP/CSK, **r** OPG/AJP/CSK; **89 t** OPG/AJP/CSK, **c** OPG/AJP/CSK, **b** OPG/AJP/CSK; **90 t** OPG/AJP/CSK, **b** OPG/AJP/CSK; **91 t** OPG/AJP/FL, **c** CI, **b** CI; **92 t** OPG/AJP/CSK; **93 t** OPG/AJP/CSK, **93 c** S, **b** CI; **94** OPG/IB; **95 t** CI, **c** S, **b** OPG/AJP/FL; **96 t** OPG/AJP/CSK, **c** CI, **b** OPG/AJP/FL; **97 t** OPG/AJP/CSK, **b** P; **98 t** CI, **b** S; **99 t** OPG/AJP/CSK, **c** CI, **b** CI; **100 t** S, **b** CI; **101 t** OPG/AJP/CSK, **cl** OPG/AJP/CSK, **cr** OPG/AJP/CSK, **b** OPG/AJP/CSK; **102** CI; **103 tl** SNY/1998 Sotheby's, Inc., **tr** CI, **c** CI, **b** OPG/AJP/CSK; **104 t** CI, **b** OPG/AJP/CSK; **105 t** S, **cl** OPG/AJP/FL, **cr** OPG/AJP/CSK, **b** OPG/AJP/CSK; **106 r** S, **b** SNY/1998 Sotheby's, Inc.; **107 t** OPG/AJP/CSK, **c** P, **b** OPG/AJP/CSK; **108** CI; **109 t** P, **c** OPG/AJP/CSK, **bl** OPG/AJP/CSK, **br** S; **110 l** OPG/AJP/CSK, **r** OPG/AJP/CSK; **111 t** S, **c** S, **b** OPG/AJP/CSK; **112 l** OPG/AJP/CSK, **r** S, **br** S; **113 t** OPG/AJP/CSK, **c** S, **b** OPG/IB; **114 bl** CI, **br** CI, **tl** OPG/AJP/CSK; **115 t** CI, **c** CI, **b** CI/CG; **116 t** OPG/AJP/CSK, **c** CI, **b** OPG/AJP/CSK; **117 t** OPG/AJP/CSK, **c** CI, **b** OPG/AJP/CSK; **118 t** OPG/IB/S, **c** OPG/AJP/CSK, **b** S; **119 tl** OPG/AJP/CSK, **r** SNY, **b** SNY; **120 l** OPG/AJP/CSK, **tr** OPG/IB, **br** OPG/AJP/CSK; **121 t** OPG/AJP/CSK, **c** OPG/AJP/CSK, **b** CI; **122 t** OPG/AJP/CSK, **b** OPG/AJP/CSK; **123 r** OPG/AJP/CSK, **tl** OPG/AJP/CSK, **bl** OPG/AJP/CSK; **124** CI; **125 t** OPG/IB/S, **cl** CI, **cr** OPG/AJP/CSK, **b** OPG/AJP/CSK; **126 t** S, **b** SNY; **127 t** OPG/AJP/CSK, **cl** CI, **cr** CI, **b** P; **128 tl** OPG/IB/S, **bl** OPG/AJP/CSK, **r** OPG/AJP/CSK; **129 r** OPG/AJP/CSK, **tl** OPG/AJP/CSK, **b** OPG/AJP/CSK; **130 l** OPG/AJP/FL; **131 t** OPG/AJP/CSK, **cl** JN/CNY, **cr** OPG/TR/A, **bl** OPG/TR/T, **br** OPG/TR/LB; **132 l** OPG/AJP/CSK, **r** CI; **133 t** OPG/TR/T, **c** OPG/AJP/CSK, **b** OPG/AJP/FL; **134 t** CI, **b** OPG/AJP/CSK; **135 t** OPG/AJP/CSK, **l** OPG/AJP/CSK, **cr** OPG/AJP/CSK, **b** OPG/SC/NH; **136** S; **137 cl** OPG/AJP/CSK, **r** S, **b** OPG/AJP/CSK; **138 t** OPG/TR/JM, **c** OPG/TR/JM, **b** OPG/AJP/CSK; **139 t** CI/CSK, **bl** OPG/TR/JM, **bc** OPG/TR/JM, **br** OPG/TR/JM; **140 t** OPG/AJP/CSK, **bl** OPG/AJP/CSK, **br** OPG/TR; **141 tl** OPG/TR, **tr** OPG/TR, **c** OPG/AJP/CSK, **b** OPG/AJP/CSK; **142** OPG/AJP/W; **143 t** OPG/AJP/CSK, **cl** CI, **cr** OPG/AJP/B, **b** OPG/AJP/CSK; **144 tl** OPG/AJP/CSK, **tr** CI/CSK, **c** OPG/AJP/CSK, **bl** CI/CSK, **br** OPG/AJP/CSK; **145 t** OPG/AJP/CSK, **cl** CI/CSK, **cr** CI/CSK, **b** OPG/AJP/CSK; **146 r** OPG/AJP/CSK, **t** OPG/AJP/W, **b** photograph©W; **147 t** P, **cl** OPG/AJP/FL, **cr** OPG/AJP/FL, **b** OPG/AJP/CSK; **148 t** SNY, **c** P, **b** OPG/AJP/CSK; **149 t** OPG/AJP/CSK, **b** P; **150 t** OPG/AJP/CSK, **b** CSK; **151 t** OPG/AJP/CSK, **tr** OPG/AJP/CSK, **cr** OPG/AJP/CSK, **b** OPG/AJP/CSK, **bl** CSK; **152 t** OPG/AJP/CSK, **bl** CSK, **r** CSK; **153 t** CSK, **bl** CSK, **br** OPG/STA/JW; **154 l** OPG, **tr** OPG/TR/LB, **b** OPG/AJP/CSK; **155 tl** CI/CSK, **tr** CI/CSK, **c** OPG/AJP/CSK, **b** CI/CSK; **156 l** B, **c** B, **r** B; **157 l** CSK, **t** OPG/AJP/B, **br** OPG/AJP/CSK; **158 l** OPG/AJP/SS, **r** OPG/AJP/CSK, **b** OPG/AJP/CSK; **159 t** OPG/NH/CS, **r** OPG/NH/SC, **b** S; **160 r** TG, **c** TG, **b** OPG/AJP/CSK; **161 tl** OPG/AJP/CSK, **tr** OPG/AJP/CSK, **bl** OPG/AJP/CSK, **br** P; **162 l** OPG/AJP/CSK, **c** OPG/IB/S, **b** OPG/AJP/CSK; **163 t** OPG/AJP/CSK, **c** OPG/P, **b** OPG/AJP; **164** OPG/JME; **165** OPG/AJP/CSK

KEY

b bottom, **c** center, **l** left, **r** right, **t** top

A Arca Antiques, Unit 351, Grays Antique Market, 58 Davies Street, London W1Y 2LP; **AB** Abode; **AJP** A.J. Photographics; **B** Bonhams, London; **CG** Christie's Geneva; **BAL** Bridgeman Art Library; **CI** Christie's Images; **CNY** Christie's New York; **CSK** Christie's South Kensington; **FL** Fay Lucas Gallery, 50 Kensington Church Street, London W8 4DA; **HJ** Hugh Johnson; **IB** Ian Booth; **IF** I. Franks, Vault 11, The London Silver Vaults, Chancery Lane, London WC2A 1QS; **JM** Jim Marshall, The Pen & Pencil Gallery, Church House, Skelton, Penrith, Cumbria CA11 9TE; **JME** James Merrell; **JN** Juliet Nusser, Christie's New York; **JW** Johnny Wachsmann, Pieces of Time, Units 17–19 Grays Antique Market, 1–7 Davies Mews, London W1Y 2LP; **LB** Lynda Brine, Assembly Antique Centre, 5–8 Saville Row, Bath BA1 2QP; **NH** Nicholas Harris; **NL** Nat Leslie Ltd., Vault 21, The London Silver Vaults, Chancery Lane, London WC2A 1QS; **OPG** Octopus Publishing Group Ltd; **P** Phillips, London; **PC** Private Collection; **PR** Piers Rankin, 15 Camden Passage, London N1 8ED; **RF** R. Feldman Ltd, Vaults 4 & 6, The London Silver Vaults, Chancery Lane, London WC2A 1QS; **S** Sotheby's Picture Library, London; **SNY** Sotheby's New York; **SS** Silstar (Antiques) Ltd, Vault 29, The London Silver Vaults, Chancery Lane, London WC2A 1QS; **ST** Stuart Chorley; **STA** Steve Tanner; **T** Tagore Ltd, Stand 302, Grays Antique Market, 58 Davies Street, London W1Y 2LP; **TG** Tadema Gallery; **TR** Tim Ridley; **W** Wartski Ltd, 14 Grafton Street, London W1X 4DE